FILIAL DEPRIVATION
AND FOSTER CARE

Filial Deprivation
and Foster Care

SHIRLEY JENKINS

AND ELAINE NORMAN

Columbia University Press

New York and London

1972

Shirley Jenkins is Professor of Social Work at the
Columbia University School of Social Work.
Elaine Norman is Research Associate at the
Columbia University School of Social Work and
former Senior Research Associate at the Com-
munity Council of Greater New York.

Copyright © 1972 Shirley Jenkins and Elaine Norman
Printed in the United States of America

Library of Congress Cataloging in Publication Data
Jenkins, Shirley.
    Filial deprivation and foster care.
    1. Foster home care.   2. Maternal deprivation.   I.
Norman, Elaine, joint author.   II. Title.
HV875.J45   362.7′33   72-3564   ISBN 0-231-03575-6

Foreword

"FAMILIES with children in foster care are families in trouble." With this first sentence Shirley Jenkins and Elaine Norman focus badly needed attention on a largely overlooked but key element in the foster care process. Traditionally, and probably understandably, emphasis has been on the child and what happens to him. It in no way diminishes the importance of the child to suggest that effective help is most unlikely without appropriate attention to the factors causing the need for foster care. As the authors see it, and as other overwhelming evidence indicates, this need stems mainly from the dysfunctioning of the family, caused primarily by the failures of our social and economic systems.

The Jenkins-Norman study is a major component of an important longitudinal child welfare research project carried out at the Columbia University School of Social Work and financed by a division of the Department of Health, Education, and Welfare. The project involves a five year follow-up of children after entry into foster care. The research has developed into separate but closely related studies of the family, the child, and the agency, with this volume focusing on the family.

The authors make clear something that should be well known and apparent, but is in truth often overlooked and disregarded. Most children enter foster care through no fault of their own, nor primarily because of individual personal problems. These do exist, of course, but all too often they have been aggravated and indeed caused by dysfunctioning of the family, resulting mainly from overwhelming environmental and social pressures. Since these pressures are all too prevalent in our society, the problems of these families are not too different from those of many other poor people. This has specific implications for what might be done in preventive care, and an important section of this book does deal with implications for policy and practice.

In focusing appropriate attention on family problems and on overall social and economic failures, the authors do not dismiss other factors. They point out that there are some children with specific needs and individual emotional problems. They also recognize that not all children can or should return to their own families, so that some will need foster care and other improved services. In discussing placements, incidentally, the authors again make clear what is so often overlooked: in many cases placement is not a carefully planned, professionally carried-out activity. All too often, it is done on an emergency, unplanned basis, with traumatic consequences for all involved.

This study can be helpful to those in the field and to all concerned with children and their families. The emphasis on families and their feelings and reactions is particularly significant. To me the implications for policy and practice are crystal clear. Unless we are prepared to do something about the social and economic problems of these families and of poor people generally, there is not much hope for progress. Major preventive programs are required that go well beyond better child welfare services. Significant changes in income maintenance policies, health care, housing, education, and employment opportunities are crucial. To say this is not to demean the importance and the value of better and more integrated child welfare or other social services. But such programs must be seen in the context of broader social and economic needs. Today it is hard to be optimistic about what will happen; but Shirley Jenkins and Elaine Norman have made a real contribution in helping to document the arguments for basic social change in policies affecting children and their families.

Mitchell I. Ginsberg, Dean
Columbia University School of Social Work

Acknowledgments

WE ARE PLEASED for the opportunity to acknowledge the contributions of many persons to our research efforts. Support of the Program for its planning year and first five years of operations, during which time data for the present volume were collected and analyzed, came from the Children's Bureau of the U.S. Department of Health, Education, and Welfare. Dr. Charles P. Gershenson, who was the Bureau's Director of Research and Evaluation, is an innovator in child welfare studies, and we are particularly grateful for his insights, creativity, and the confidence he maintained in our research. We are also appreciative of continuing support during the last two years from the Community Services Administration, Social and Rehabilitation Service, and their Office of Research and Demonstrations.

The study has been housed at the Columbia University School of Social Work, and we have had encouragement over the years from Mitchell I. Ginsberg, Dean, Sidney Berengarten, Associate Dean, and Samuel Finestone,

Director of the Center for Research and Demonstration. We have worked closely and cooperatively with our colleagues on the companion Child Welfare Research Program, of which Dr. David Fanshel is Director. On our own study there have been important contributions from staff, in particular Mallory Pepper, Research Associate, who supervised two field interviews, identified qualitative material for use in several chapters, and prepared the index for this volume. Dr. Leonard S. Kogan, Research Consultant, has been unfailingly helpful, wise, and supportive.

A field study, involving a large sample of people with critical problems, would not have been possible without the cooperation of various agencies responsible for service delivery. We wish to express particular appreciation to Elizabeth C. Beine, Director of the Bureau of Child Welfare, New York City Department of Social Services, and to her coworkers, and to the Hon. Florence M. Kelley, Administrative Judge, Family Court of the State of New York, and Marion M. Brennan, Deputy Director of Probation, Office of Probation for the courts of New York City, for their assistance in providing access to the study sample. Personnel in over 70 agencies cooperated extensively with our study staff and we are grateful for that cooperation. The Advisory Committee to the Child Welfare and Family Welfare Research Programs was helpful in numerous ways, particularly in reflecting the needs and concerns of the child welfare field.

Our staff of social work interviewers collected the basic data for analysis, and worked with skill, sensitivity, and professional integrity. Finally, we are grateful to the natural parents of the children and the mothers, fathers, and relatives who participated in lengthy interviews in their homes in response to the following request: "We want to get information to help make better services available to children and families." The contribution of these respondents was freely given, and we hope our findings and interpretations will make the gift relationship worthwhile.

New York   Shirley Jenkins and Elaine Norman
April 1972

Contents

63287

FILIAL DEPRIVATION
AND FOSTER CARE

CHAPTER ONE

Families in Need

FAMILIES with children in foster care are families in trouble. Their personal lives are disrupted, and they face difficult social and economic circumstances. These families come to the attention of the community primarily through the network of child welfare agencies, which assume the social role of caring for dependent children. The heavy responsibility of fulfilling this task has meant that the traditional focus of the foster care field has largely been child rather than family centered. This approach, however, may no longer be appropriate or effective. The majority of children who enter foster care do so through no fault of their own, or even because of identifiable individual problems. They enter care as the legatees of family difficulties, of disrupted parenting patterns, and of dysfunction within a social system in which the problems of raising children are intensified by environmental pressures, so that this task, although assumed to be a family function, cannot always be effectively carried out by the family unit.

The needs of the placed children reflect the needs of their

total family constellations. Furthermore, the families themselves are not an atypical group in urban society today; they merge with and become almost indistinguishable from others on the urban poverty scene. The majority of them have characteristics which have been repeatedly reported to be descriptive of inner-city minority residents. A disproportionate percentage of children in foster care are from families of black and Puerto Rican parentage; to a great extent they come from female-headed households; and they have experienced living conditions below the poverty line. In the majority of cases the adults in the families have known long-term economic deprivation, and have below-average education and above-average pathology. They have problems of mental and physical illness and have experienced and expressed the alienation, disturbance, violence, and abuse commonly seen in the larger society.

When children come to the attention of the child welfare agencies, the multiplicity of problems in their histories arouses professional concern for family needs and problems. Too often, however, there are limited resources for services to the families, and there is frequently an understandable inclination toward directing what resources are available to the young. Often the rationale is that there may be more payoff in insulating the children and raising them away from their homes until they can establish new and hopefully healthier families of their own. This appears to be an easier task than attempting rehabilitation of their natural parents. Although it is tempting to direct attention exclusively to the young, since this simplifies the immediate problems of service delivery, in fact such a model can be no more than an interim palliative. The majority of children return to their former homes and communities after foster care. In addition, the social environment which contributed to their problems continues to produce new child populations who suffer similar deprivations.

The focus of the present study on the families of children in foster care is directed to the conditions which give rise to the need for care, as well as to the interactions among child, family, and environment from an ecological perspective. Certain exceptions to the emphasis on poverty as a backdrop to foster care should be noted. Not all children in foster care come from deprived circumstances or minority groups: some enter care for reasons of personal child need, emotional problems, extreme unforeseen emergencies, or neglect and abuse unrelated to socioeconomic situations. Furthermore, not all children do or even should return to their natural families; indeed, for some children their best interests may be served by a childhood in placement. A differentiated approach is needed. The present study of natural families, their characteristics, composition, socioeconomic status, attitudes, feelings, behavior, and expectations is intended to present a frame of reference from which preventive services in behalf of children can be developed realistically. For the residual caseload of children for whom long-term placement is essential, the locus of placement and nature of services must be based on their total needs.

This study of families is one component of a longitudinal research program begun in 1964 at the Columbia University School of Social Work. The study was initiated under the sponsorship of the Child Welfare Research and Demonstration Grants Program of the Children's Bureau of the U.S. Department of Health, Education, and Welfare. Subsequently the program was transferred to the Division of Child Welfare Research and Demonstrations, Office of Research and Demonstrations of the Social and Rehabilitation Service.

Following a planning year, the overall study, initially known as the Child Welfare Research Program, selected a sample of 624 children in New York City who came into foster care in 1966. This cohort consisted of boys and girls who entered initial placement between January and November 1966, including children from birth through 12 years of age, closely proportionate in age and sex to the population of such children in foster care at that time. To become part of the study group, the children must have remained in care for a minimum of 90 days following entry into placement, thus restricting the sample to children in long-term care. A maximum of two children per family was included in the sample, these two being selected at random from siblings who met the eligibility criteria. The study design was predicated on a five-year follow-up after entry into care, regardless of whether the child remained in placement or was discharged before the end of the projected study period.

Following an initial analysis of the patterns of entry into care, the longitudinal research evolved into separate but interrelated studies along three main lines: the family, the child, and the agency. In 1970 the overall program was subdivided, the Family Welfare Research Program and the Child Welfare Research Program continuing with independent but parallel research. Separate reports of findings from initial data collection procedures are being made for each study phase. The present volume presents findings on families.[1] Follow-up studies have been subsequently undertaken

1. Other volumes reporting research data will be published subsequently by Columbia University Press. The volume on children will be pre-

both on families whose children remained in care and on those whose children were discharged during the five-year period. Data from these follow-up interviews will be reported in a later volume. Child, family, and agency data will also be interrelated subsequently both over time and across study domains in order to present an integrated picture of the overall nature and consequences of long-term foster care.

STUDY METHOD

Primary attention was focused on the 467 family groups which parented the 624 sample children. The differences in these numbers is accounted for by the 157 cases in which two children from one family were included in the sample. The figure of 467 becomes the basic "N" for the family study, but this total can by no means be construed as representing stable, intact family constellations. Data on familial and extrafamilial relationships, as well as on living and child-caring arrangements, will indicate the complex internal and external problems which beset these families.

A major myth in the literature on foster placements is that such placements are the result of carefully considered decisions in which trained social workers help families with special problems and plan for substitute care. This model, in fact, is seen in only a small percentage of cases. For the majority of children and their families, placement is an emergency, an unplanned, traumatic experience, and full knowledge of why children come into care cannot be found in the entry records. To gather relevant data, to compre-

---

pared by Drs. David Fanshel and Eugene B. Shinn, and the agency study by Dr. Deborah Shapiro.

hend parents' perceptions of their own situations, to probe into their feelings and attitudes, direct access to families is needed. The family study utilized home interviews with mothers and fathers as its primary data collection procedure. If natural parents were not accessible, substitute child-caring persons, such as close relatives, were seen. These initial interviews were conducted as soon as possible after the child entered the study sample, which was 90 days after entry into foster care.

Undertaking face-to-face interviews in the family members' own homes allowed for exploration of sensitive, emotion-laden material and tended to produce greater candidness and depth of response than would a written questionnaire, an office interview, or a study of records alone. In addition, by conducting interviews in homes, interviewers had an opportunity to observe and describe living conditions, as well as to get a sense of the climate of family interaction. The staff members conducting home interviews were trained, experienced social workers. Their specialized professional background equipped them not only to draw on information in sensitive areas, but also to handle appropriately any extreme reactions or distress which might arise in the interview situation. Several of the social worker interviewers were bilingual, and almost one-fourth of the interviews were conducted in Spanish.[2]

CONTENT AREAS. In the family interview five major content areas were explored: (1) experiences leading to placement, including the reason for placement and events surrounding placement; (2) parental feelings with regard to

2. In order to insure uniformity of question wording, a Spanish translation of the interview schedule was utilized in these cases.

6

placement, particularly parental feelings on the day the child entered foster care; (3) experiences after placement, including changes in adult life situations and in contacts with the child; (4) generalized parental social attitudes and values, including child-rearing attitudes, ideas on desirable child traits, attitudes toward social agencies, general social orientation, role preferences and performances, and expectations for self and child; and (5) social and economic background, including family history, socioeconomic circumstances, and other demographic characteristics. The interview schedule combined several types of question format. Open-ended questions designed to encourage free responses were included, as well as closed questions forcing a choice of predetermined categories. There were checklists on which only agreement or disagreement could be noted and sentence completion tasks calling for spontaneous and projective responses.

The opening approach to mothers and fathers was to ask them why their child(ren) had entered foster care. Positioned at the beginning of the interview, this question immediately focused respondents on the problem which brought them within the scope of the study. Since this was a story most parents knew well and were anxious to tell, they answered readily, and this facilitated interaction between respondent and interviewer. More importantly, the information itself was crucial material, since reason for placement is a major variable differentiating groups within the foster care population.[3]

3. See Shirley Jenkins and Mignon Sauber, *Paths to Child Placement, Family Situations Prior to Foster Care* (Community Council of Greater New York, 1966). In this study of preplacement factors for 891 foster children, categories describing the main reason for placement were de-

Several factors related to the reason for placement were then explored in the interview, including contributing problems and their timing, source of the idea to place the child, differences of opinion on the advisability of placement, attempts to make alternative child care arrangements, typical sources of family help, and extent and nature both of preparation of the child for placement and of help for the parent in accepting the separation. Some of these probes were descriptive of the situational factors relating to placement; others were designed to uncover motivation and feelings.

The interview continued by exploring a major concept in the study, "filial deprivation," or the feelings experienced by a parent when separated from his or her child. Substantial attention has been given in the child welfare field to the impact on children of separation from parents. Little systematic research has been done, however, in exploring the feelings and reactions of parents, in particular mothers, who undergo long-term separation from children. In this study the specific series of questions on filial deprivation began by asking the respondent how he or she felt the day the child was placed. Probes following this initial question explored whether the respondent would have felt differently if the child were being cared for by a relative, a friend, or a homemaker, rather than an agency. Differences in reactions to placement in a child care institution or in a foster home were noted. In order to relate feelings to actions and to help nonverbal respondents express themselves, questions were asked about precise activities of respondents on the day of placement. Finally, a checklist of feelings developed

---

veloped, and these were utilized in the present research, with some modifications.

from pretest interviews was completed, with each parent reporting specific feelings as well as the associated feeling objects or referents.

Once a child has been placed in foster care, the question arises as to whether the family begins to "close in" behind him, with the parents arranging their lives in such a way as to discourage the possibility of the child returning home. Several questions in the interview explored changes in parental feelings after separation, as well as changes in life situations of families, and a series of incomplete sentences was included as a projective device to explore parental reactions to mothering and fathering.

The interview evaluated six areas of parental attitudes and values. The first area related to child rearing and was designed to differentiate parents on an authoritarian-permissive continuum. Parents made choices between paired items, both alternatives being socially acceptable, and on subjects related to discipline, training, and behavior. The second attitudinal area explored parental choices of desirable child traits. The task comprised ranking child attributes according to parental priorities. The results indicated which child traits were most valued by parents.

The third attitudinal area included in the interview was designed to study the parents' reactions to social agencies, in particular foster care agencies, on three dimensions: (1) as facilitators of child care, helping families in time of need; (2) as usurpers of parental rights; or (3) as surrogates who appropriately assume a continuing responsibility for child care. Generalized attitudes reflecting the respondents' views of society were next explored. These dealt with three aspects of social orientation: (1) alienation; (2) calculativeness; and (3) trust.

9

Parental role expectations and performances comprised the fifth attitudinal area in the interview. Nine family-related tasks, three traditionally performed by women, three traditionally performed by men, and three usually performed by both, were presented to respondents, and each was asked both "who should do" the task in a two-parent family and "who actually does" the task in their own households. Findings differentiated between actual role performances and idealized role expectations held by the respondents. Since responses came from both mothers and fathers, differences between male and female concepts were also analyzed.

The final section in the attitudinal area related to goals and aspirations. Parents were asked what level of education and what occupation they desired for their children, and also what were their own primary wishes in three areas. Their responses indicated both aspiration levels and value orientation.

The last major content area in the interview schedule was designed to collect data about the social and economic situations of families. This area included three categories: family history, socioeconomic circumstances, and demographic characteristics. The family history sequence requested information on the childhood experiences of the respondents themselves, including whether they had been in foster care placement themselves, and on any history of family pathology. In the social and economic categories data were sought on the amount and source of family income, the educational attainment of the best-educated adult in the household, and the quality of housing and neighborhood of residence. A socioeconomic index was developed to differentiate within the study population. Demographic data such as age, ethnic group, religion, and marital status were also gathered. The utilization of trained social workers as research interviewers made it feasible to include their professional judgments on family situations and placement in the interview findings.[4]

INTERVIEW PROCEDURES. In order to explore relevant concepts in the research, particularly in the area of filial deprivation, and in order to test the effectiveness of the planned interview, three pretest operations were undertaken before beginning large-scale field interviewing. During the winter of 1965–1966, seven exploratory group interviews were held with parents of children in care but not in the study sample. These group interviews took place in the offices of social agencies, and they focused primarily on the feelings these parents had had when their children were placed. Group interaction among mothers and fathers proved particularly conducive to eliciting responses in variety and depth. The group interviews were tape recorded, and a content analysis of the tapes was utilized in the development of the filial deprivation section of the final study questionnaire.

In addition to the group interviews, there were individual exploratory interviews with non-sample cases in comparable circumstances.[5] These sessions, which were open ended

4. Some initial findings in the areas of family circumstances, attitudes, and parental expectations have been discussed in Shirley Jenkins and Elaine Norman, "Families of Children in Foster Care," *Children,* July–August 1969, pp. 155–59.
5. Results of one aspect of the exploratory phase of interview construction were reported in Dorothy E. Barnes et al., *An Exploratory Study into Methods of Evaluating Filial Deprivation* (unpublished Student

and allowed for free expression of parental views, provided clues for developing relevant question areas. Finally, the completed interview schedule was subjected to field testing by the professional interview staff. Interviewer reactions to the pretest and an analysis of response patterns to different questions were used to revise the schedule prior to full field operations, which began in May 1966.

The interviews, which were conducted in the homes of the natural parents, took an average of two hours to complete. The reaction of the respondents to being interviewed was on the whole favorable. Initial reactions of parents when first approached by family interviewers ranged from outright eagerness at the prospect of being interviewed to fear and suspicion. In the great majority of cases, once the interview began, respondents who were initially apprehensive became involved and cooperative. The diverse ethnic backgrounds of the interviewers, their bilingual skills, and knowledge of neighborhood conditions, were crucial in the successful completion of the family interviews.

During the field operations both research staff and social work interviewers were concerned with procedures to safeguard confidentiality and the rights of respondents to privacy. The nature of the research necessitated access to the personal affairs of respondents, as well as to their actions, thoughts, and feelings. The use of the interview method meant that such data were obtained only with the informed consent of the participants. Each respondent was told about the nature and the purpose of the research study and asked to participate in it voluntarily. Of all persons approached

Group Master's Project, New York, Columbia University School of Social Work, May 1966).

only about 5 percent refused to be interviewed. Furthermore, during the course of the interview, respondents were reminded that they were free to forego answering any particular question area. However, such requests were rarely made. Information about individuals secured during the field operations, from current addresses to personal attitudes, was not shared with any other person or agency. There were periodic meetings of the interview staff to discuss problems of privacy and confidentiality and to work out strategies to overcome difficulties. Although these sessions added time and effort to the interview procedures, they were important not only in safeguarding respondents' rights but also in helping the interview staff work out its role and its responsibilities to both the research and the client.

STUDY SAMPLE

There were many difficulties in locating and communicating with parents who were experiencing both personal and environmental crises. This was primarily a poverty population, with high mobility in housing, low educational levels, and a high percentage of non-English-speaking members. Furthermore, the children typically entered care at a time of crisis or change, often because parents were unable to carry on their parental roles. Considering this background, the ratio of success in the field interviews was very high; 91 percent of all attempted interviews were completed.

Although the overall sample included 467 families, the family study attempted interviews in only 430 cases. Thirty-seven cases were therefore excluded from field operations. In 26 of these excluded cases, adoptions of the sample children were pending, and research interviews were considered inappropriate because of possible effect on the adoptive planning process. The remaining 11 cases were those in which the concerned agencies or the Court requested that no interview be conducted for casework reasons. All agencies had been informed of the research and given an opportunity to ask that any case be excluded, but this occurred only in these 11 cases.

For the 430 attempted interviews, at least one parent or substitute in 390 families was successfully reached. In 19 cases interviewers were unable to locate any family member or knowledgeable respondent, even after extensive search (in some cases including up to 10 attempts at home visits). The remaining 21 cases were families which refused to cooperate in the research and did not wish to be interviewed.

Initial decisions on preferred respondents were made prior to the field interview, and in all cases it was considered preferable that priority be given to the natural mother of the sample child. If she was not available and the father was, he was seen. If neither natural parent was available, a parent surrogate was interviewed. This was defined as an individual who either took full-time care of the child for a minimum of three months prior to placement, or who typically shared child care responsibility with the natural parent. In most cases the parent surrogate was a grandparent. As a final alternative, if none of the above was available, an informant who had knowledge of the child, the family, and the placement situation (e.g., another relative) was seen. In the initial interview round, 297 mothers, 49 fathers, 24 parent surrogates (mainly grandparents), and 20 informants were interviewed. It should be noted, however, that not all sections of the questionnaire were used for parent surrogates—e.g., questions on maternal and paternal attitudes were not appropriate—but factual information was obtained. Table I.1 shows the "response rates" in the field interviewing operations in the family study.

Upon completion of the initial interview, which took place from May 1966 to April 1967 and included primarily mother respondents, it was apparent that inclusion of a higher representation of fathers in interview data would contribute substantially to better understanding of family conditions and attitudes. As a result, a special father interview was conducted and completed between April and July 1967. Unlike the procedure with respect to mothers, however, no attempt was made to interview all fathers in the sample. Many fathers were, in fact, totally unknown. In addition, a high incidence of pathology in the paternal population indicated the necessity of careful screening before ap-

TABLE I.1

Number of Families Interviewed

	Number of families	Related number of children
Total number of cases in study	*467*	*624*
Excluded cases	37	41
Adoption	26	26
Agency or Court	11	15
Total cases in field operations	*430*	*583*
Number interviewed	390	533
Number not interviewed	40	50
Refusal	21	23
Unable to locate	19	27

proaching this group. It was considered essential to inform each mother of the prospective father interview and give her the opportunity to ask that the father not be visited. The father was not seen if objections were raised by the mother, in particular when she expressed concern about possible consequences for herself or the child or fear of reprisals. In some cases fathers had no knowledge at all of the placement, and it would not have been appropriate for the research to function as informant.

Forty-nine fathers had already been interviewed in the initial field operation, because of inability to locate or interview the mother. Efforts were made to interview an additional 167 fathers, and of these, 88 were seen. Together with the earlier respondents, a total of 137 natural fathers of the study sample were interviewed, as well as the 297 mothers. This refers to the full field interview. For purposes of analysis, demographic data were obtained, where available, on all parents of children in the sample, so that factors such as age and birthplace were incorporated in the data for almost all mothers and fathers of the 390 cases, even if no personal interview was obtained.

In order to understand the variations in sample size which are referred to in reporting various aspects of the study findings, certain key distinctions must be noted. (1) The difference between number of families and number of children is based on the fact that some sample children had siblings who were also in the study. (2) There is a difference between numbers of mothers and fathers interviewed. This resulted from uneven availability of mothers and fathers, as well as the consent factor, which meant mothers, if available, had to agree that fathers be seen. (In a total of 88 cases, both the mother and the father of the sample child were interviewed.) (3) There is a difference between total number in the overall sample and the number actually interviewed. This is explained by such case reasons as lack of inclusion in field operations, refusals, and inability to locate. (4) Certain categories of data have different bases because of the nature of the material. Thus, maternal and paternal attitude data could only be collected when there was direct access to the respondent, who reported her or his own reactions and feelings. Such data were not collected if the respondent was a surrogate parent or informant.

Socioeconomic data were collected on households in which the child, the interviewed mother, and the interviewed father resided just prior to the child's entrance into foster care. In many cases there were actually three different households, and so three different sets of socioeconomic data were collected. If the child, the mother, or the father was hospitalized or institutionalized at the time of placement, no household information was collected for that particular respondent. In fact, 61 children, 57 interviewed mothers, and 8 interviewed fathers were hospitalized or institutionalized just prior to placement. For the children, this refers primarily to babies who were placed directly from the hospital in which they were born. Excluding such cases, and taking this into account, socioeconomic data about households of children are based on 329 cases, while mother households and father households include 240 and 129 cases, respectively.

In the presentation of findings which follows, the demographic and socioeconomic characteristics of the study sample are first described, followed by data on the preplacement situations and on reasons for placement. Feelings of parents on the day the child entered care are analyzed, as are parental attitudes and values. Family situations in the months directly after placement are also described. A special analysis is made of responses of "parent pairs," based on the 88 cases in which interviews were carried out with both the natural mother and the natural father of the same child. The interrelationships among the various categories of research data are explored, and the analysis concludes by presenting the critical social policy issues raised by the study findings.

CHAPTER TWO

Family Characteristics
and Circumstances

CHILDREN do not come into care because their parents are poor or black or sick. If that were the case, the numbers in care would be many times larger than they actually are. For most households poverty is a necessary but not a sufficient condition for placement. It is the marginal family, whose characteristics and social circumstances are such that it cannot sustain further stress, which utilizes the placement system as a last resort when its own fragile supports break down. The major exception to this pattern is the situation of the emotionally disturbed child who is placed in a residential treatment center. Such children are frequently white and middle class. The large majority of families in New York City with children in care, however, are in deprived circumstances.

Study findings show that, just prior to being placed in foster care, most of the children in the study sample lived in impoverished households located in the poorest neighborhoods of New York City. Approximately one-half of these households were being supported by public assistance. For those families where there was salaried income, earnings averaged under $100 a week. Field visits and observations by social workers indicated that, in a sizable number of cases, the apartments and buildings in which the children lived contained such health and safety hazards as rats, roaches, garbage littering the halls, rotting floors, poor light, poor ventilation, inadequate heat, and inadequate hot water.

The natural parents of the children in care were young, typically in their twenties and thirties. Only about half of the parents were married to each other and, even when married, few were living together. Most of the children's parents were born in the South of the United States or in Puerto Rico. The number of years of completed education was considerably below the national average.

In this chapter detailed demographic and socioeconomic descriptions of the study families will be presented. Personal characteristics of the families will be noted as well as data on income, housing, and neighborhood living conditions. The special factors which distinguish these families from the general New York City population will be identified. Finally, a socioeconomic scale specifically constructed to differentiate within the sample, which is relatively economically homogeneous, will be presented. This scale, developed for the purposes of the present research, is designed to provide a socioeconomic score for each family, which will then be related to other variables and characteristics in the study, including attitudes, feelings, and preplacement experiences.

NEW YORK CITY POPULATION
AND THE STUDY POPULATION:
SOME CRITICAL VARIABLES

Comparison of the families whose children entered foster care in 1966 with the total 1966 population of New York City is complicated by the fact that population data for New York City for that year are based primarily on projections of 1960 census material. Because there are many unknowns involved, it is very difficult to make accurate population projections from data collected six years earlier. In order to minimize error in identifying factors which distinguish the families in the study from the total New York City population, the comparisons which were made on several critical variables utilized both projections and sample surveys as sources of population data.

The New York City Department of Health birth statistics [1] are accurate records of children born in New York City hospitals. Estimates of the child population of New York City in any given year from these data, however, do not take migration information into account, which is significant for both the Puerto Rican population and the migrant groups from the South. A second source of data is that used by the New York City Planning Commission.[2] These data are based on projections of the 1960 census and are available for the year 1965. Such projections take into account postulated trends in migration and birth rates. The

1. New York City Department of Health, Bureau of Records and Statistics, *Birth Records 1954–1966*.
2. New York City Department of City Planning, *1965 Population for 300 Planning Areas* (New York, 1965).

postulated trends, however, have not been verified. The other source of data used is the Population Health Survey.[3] Its estimates of New York City noninstitutional population size and characteristics are generated from an annual survey of a randomly selected cluster sample of New York City households. Since each source of data noted above has limitations, information from all three was used to reach an adequate basis for comparison of the study sample with the population of the city as a whole.

Regardless of which source is utilized, it can be readily seen that many of the demographic characteristics of the study sample are those which have typically linked children with poverty. Three are of particular relevance: ethnic group, level of income, and percent of female-headed households.

ETHNIC GROUP. In defining the poverty population, Orshansky identified ethnic group as one characteristic descriptive of the nation's poor in 1966, the year the study sample entered care. She stated, "it is . . . a fact that non-whites made up about one-third of the nation's poor in 1966, compared with just over one-fourth in 1959—a widening disadvantage explained only in small part by the greater population growth among non-whites." [4] With regard to ethnic distribution, the study sample is widely divergent

3. Leonard S. Kogan and M. J. Wantman, *Estimates of Population Characteristics, New York City, 1964–1965–1966* (Population Health Survey, Center for Social Research, The City University of New York, Report No. RB-P4-68, 1968).

4. Mollie Orshansky, "The Shape of Poverty in 1966," in *Children's Allowances and the Economic Welfare of Children,* ed. Eveline M. Burns (New York, Citizens' Committee for Children of New York, Inc., 1968), p. 23.

from the total population of New York City. As seen in Table II.1, the three population data sources estimate, for example, that from 56 to 65 percent of all New York City children in 1965–1966 were white. By contrast, only 31 percent of the study sample of placed children were white. A comparison of the ethnic distribution by families, rather than by children, yields even sharper differences. Black and Puerto Rican families are nearly three times more prevalent in the study sample than they are in the general population.[5]

Since the study children were a sample drawn from all children entering care in 1966, a relevant question is whether the ethnic distribution of those children differed significantly from the total population of all children in foster care at that time. From the monthly population reports of the Bureau of Child Welfare it was determined that on December 31, 1966 there was a total of 22,886 children in care in New York City.[6] Of this number, 30 percent were white, 47 percent black, and 23 percent Puerto Rican. This percentage distribution differs negligibly from that of the sample children, whose corresponding distribution is 31 percent white, 45 percent black, and 24 percent Puerto Rican.

Two conclusions can be drawn from these data. Ethnic

5. As noted, the study sample included a maximum of two placed children from any one family. Thus, the family with larger numbers of offspring tends to be underrepresented in the child sample, which is based on number of children placed. The larger families are more likely to be black or Puerto Rican.
6. New York City, Department of Welfare (Department of Social Services), Bureau of Child Welfare, *Summary Analysis of Monthly Population Reports Submitted by Foster Care Agencies, Children Remaining in Care on December 31, 1966.*

TABLE II.1

Percent Distribution of Children and Families
in New York City and in Study Sample, by Ethnic Group
Based on Three Data Sources

| | | Ethnic group | | |
	Total	White	Non-white[a]	Puerto Rican[b]
CHILDREN, BIRTH TO 12 YEARS				
All New York City children				
Population Health Survey, 1966 (N = 1,626,500)	100	56	24	20
Department of City Planning, 1965[c] (N = 1,579,368)	100	62	25	13
Department of Health, 1966 (N = 1,979,212)	100	65	21	14
Study sample children				
Total children (N = 624)	100	31	45	24
Children of interviewed families (N = 533)[d]	100	24	43	33
FAMILIES				
All New York City families				
Population Health Survey, 1966 (N = 2,080,000)	100	74	17	9
Study sample families				
Total families interviewed (N = 390)	100	24	44	32

[a] Blacks comprise over 90 percent of "non-whites" in the population estimates. All "non-whites" in the present study sample are black.

[b] "Puerto Rican" includes both white and black persons who were born in Puerto Rico or had at least one parent born there.

[c] Adjusted proportionally for the 10 to 15-year-old age group.

[d] The exclusion of pending adoptive cases from family interviews resulted in a somewhat smaller percentage of white and a larger percentage of Puerto Rican children in the interviewed group than in the overall sample.

distribution of children in the sample corresponded almost exactly to that of all children in foster care. On the other hand, regardless of which of the three sources of estimated population is utilized as a basis for comparison, there is a sharp disparity between the ethnic group distribution of placed children and their families and that in the city as a whole. For the placing population, there was substantial underrepresentation of white families and overrepresentation of both black and Puerto Rican families.

SOURCE AND AMOUNT OF INCOME. Perhaps the strongest contrast between families in the study sample and the New York City population is with regard to source of income. In December 1966 the Department of Social Services (formerly the Department of Welfare) estimated that 7.9 percent of the population of New York City was receiving public assistance.[7] By comparison, in the study sample of the same year 45 percent of the households from which the children were placed were supported primarily by public assistance at the time of placement.[8] In an additional 7 percent of cases supplementary public assistance was being received in addition to other income. Thus, the total number of households in the sample receiving some form of public assistance just before their children entered care was 52 percent. Those families which were receiving assistance had usually been receiving it for many years, indicating patterns of

7. New York City Department of Welfare, *The Welfarer*, XIX, No. 3 (March 1967).
8. Children from 61 interviewed families were placed directly from the hospital in which they were born or from an institution. Data on living conditions were not available for those cases. Consequently, the sample size for children's households with reported socioeconomic variables equals 329 rather than 390.

chronic dependency. As shown in Table II.2 37 percent of the study homes receiving welfare had been receiving that help for six years or more. Only 14 percent had received assistance for less than one year. The median length of time public assistance had been received by the group of welfare recipients was 4.9 years prior to placement. Since children in the sample ranged from birth through 12 years, this corresponded fairly closely with the age of the average child.

Table II.3 presents results on the main sources of support for the study families. Forty-three percent of the households in the sample were supported primarily by income from the salaries of working members. An additional 7 percent of households lived primarily on income from sources other than salaries or public assistance, such as benefit or insurance payments, alimony, child support, or help from friends or relatives. One percent of the households had no established source of income, and the main source of support was not ascertainable for the remaining 4 percent.

TABLE II.2

Length of Time Public Assistance Was Received in Recipient
Study Households Prior to Placement
(N = 171)

Length of time public assistance received	Percent distribution
Less than one year	14
One to less than three years	18
Three years to less than six years	17
Six years or more	37
Not ascertainable	14
Total	100

TABLE II.3

Main Source of Support in Study Households
Just Prior to Placement
(N = 329)

Main source of support	Percent distribution
Public assistance	45[a]
Salaries	43
Other source	7
Benefits	4
Alimony or child support	2
Help from friends or relatives	1
No established income	1
Not ascertainable	4
Total	100

[a] An additional 7 percent of households were receiving public assistance as a supplementary rather than a main source of support.

Those families in the study sample who were not receiving public assistance as either the main or a supplementary source of support had an estimated median income of $85 a week, or $4,420 per year (based on Table II.4). Considering the fact that the number of persons in the typical study household was 4.8,[9] the median income for study families which were not receiving public assistance corresponded roughly to the poverty level for a non-farm family of four in 1966, which the United States Government placed at $3,335.[10] The study median is substantially lower

9. There was no discernible difference in number of persons per household according to main source of support, e.g., salaries, benefits, or public assistance.
10. Orshansky, "The Shape of Poverty in 1966," p. 21.

TABLE II.4

Amount of Weekly Income Just Prior to Placement
in Study Households Not Receiving Public Assistance[a]

(N = 158)

Amount of weekly income	Percent distribution
Under $50 a week	12
$50 to under $75 a week	16
$75 to under $100 a week	25
$100 to under $125 a week	13
$125 a week or over	13
No established income	2
Income not ascertainable	19
Total	*100*

[a] As either main or supplementary source of support.

than the Population Health Survey estimate of median family income in New York City in 1966, which was $6,684.[11]

Receipt of public assistance as a main or a supplementary source of support indicates a level of living that can be designated as "subsistence" or "poverty." [12] Fifty-two percent of the families were receiving such assistance. An additional 14 percent of families were not receiving public

11. Kogan, *Estimates of Population Characteristics*, p. 13. The Population Health Survey estimates are for families with all sources of support, including public assistance.

12. The actual dollar income of families on welfare is difficult to report because of fluctuating family size and disparity in rent among households. The typical Aid to Families of Dependent Children monthly payment in New York City in 1966, however, for a family of four, including rent allotment, was $257.75, or approximately $3,100 a year. See New York City Department of Welfare (presently Department of Social Services), *Basic Department of Welfare Monthly Allowances Effective July 1, 1966* (prepared by Home Economics Program).

aid but had household incomes of less than $3,900 a year. It is possible to estimate grossly, therefore, that approximately two-thirds of the study families lived at or below the poverty level. Only 6 percent of these families had incomes at or above $6,500 annually, or slightly below the estimated citywide median.

As seen in Table II.5, there were differences among the

TABLE II.5

Level of Income in Study Households
Just Prior to Placement, by Ethnic Group

| | | Ethnic group (percent distribution) | | |
| | Total (N = 329) | White (N = 74) | Black (N = 141) | Puerto Rican (N = 114) |
Level of income[a]				
Household income less than $3,900 a year and all public assistance recipients	66	38	72	74
Household income $3,900 to less than $6,500 a year	19	31	14	18
Household income $6,500 or more a year	6	12	4	5
No established income	1	1	1	—
Income not ascertainable	8	18	9	3
Total	100	100	100	100

[a] The three levels of income in the table reflect the "poverty range," the range "above poverty but below adequate," and "adequate but moderate" circumstances, respectively. The rationale for these categories is discussed in the text.

proportions of families in different ethnic groups in terms of economic level. White families were least likely to be living below the poverty level and most likely to have incomes at or above the citywide median. A further analysis of the data, not shown in the table, indicates differences in proportion of families receiving public assistance by ethnic group. Only 20 percent of the white families were receiving welfare just before placement occurred, as compared with 62 percent of Puerto Rican families and 60 percent of black families.

Puerto Rican households on welfare had been receiving such help for the longest period of time, as compared to the other ethnic groups. Of those families who were welfare clients, 62 percent of the Puerto Ricans and 53 percent of the blacks had been receiving assistance for three years or more, as shown in Table II.6. Of the 15 white families who were on public assistance, only four had been recipients for three years or more.

TABLE II.6

Length of Time on Public Assistance of Recipient Study Households Just Prior to Placement, by Ethnic Group

Time public assistance received	Ethnic group (percent distribution)			
	Total (N = 171)	White (N = 15)	Black (N = 85)	Puerto Rican (N = 71)
Less than three years	32	46	34	26
Three years or more	54	27	53	62
Not ascertainable	14	27	13	12
Total	100	100	100	100

HOUSING AND NEIGHBORHOOD. Any description of housing in a metropolis like New York, with a deteriorated inner
city, must take into account not only the particular dwellings of families but also the conditions of neighborhoods in
which they live. There are numerous indicators for evaluating neighborhood milieu, and these tend to repeat and re-
inforce each other. Two variables, income level and juvenile
delinquency rate, give substantial information about neighborhood conditions and are highly correlated with other socioeconomic indicators.

In a study based on 1960 data, 74 neighborhoods in
New York City were ranked on several indexes, including
median family income and juvenile delinquency rate.[13] The
highest- and lowest-ranking neighborhoods had median
family incomes of $9,700 and $3,700 per year, respectively. The lowest juvenile delinquency rate for any neighborhood was 8 delinquents per 1,000 youth, and the highest rate was 101 delinquents per 1,000 youth. Within these
ranges, the average family in the present study lived in a
neighborhood which had below-average median income,
$5,000 a year, and above-average delinquency rate, 63 per
1,000 youth. Two-thirds of the households from which the
children were placed were located in the 20 neighborhoods
in New York City which had the highest juvenile delinquency rates and the lowest family incomes.

Ethnic group continued to be an associated factor. Residence in these 20 "poverty neighborhoods" was the case for
approximately four-fifths of the Puerto Rican households,
about three-quarters of the black households, and only

one-quarter of the white households (see Table II.7).

In addition to neighborhoods, the housing units in which the children lived were studied. After a review of standards for dwellings and consultation with specialists in the housing field, a list of 21 items reflecting conditions dangerous to health and safety was prepared by the study staff. The existence of those conditions in the dwelling units where sample children had lived just prior to placement was ascertained through observation by staff interviewers and from reports of family members. Only 19 percent of the study households contained none of the 21 negative conditions. The remaining households had an average of 5 negative housing conditions. Twenty-two percent of the dwelling units were indicated as having rats, for example, 20 percent had rotting apartment floors, and 20 percent had garbage littering the building halls. Details are shown in Table II.8.

This picture of living circumstances of families whose children entered placement is not data intended to show a

TABLE II.7

Study Households Situated in "Poverty Neighborhoods" in New York City, by Ethnic Group

Ethnic group	Percent of households in 20 neighborhoods with lowest median family income	Percent of households in 20 neighborhoods with highest juvenile delinquency rates
White (N = 74)	30	25
Black (N = 141)	74	73
Puerto Rican (N = 114)	82	77
Total (N = 329)	67	63

TABLE II.8

Negative Housing Conditions in Study Households
Just Prior to Placement (N = 329)

Negative condition:[a]	Percent of households with condition
No telephone	54
Roaches	53
Falling plaster in apartment	34
Noticeably dirty floors in building halls	24
Rats	22
Falling plaster in building halls	20
Garbage littering building halls	20
Rotting floors in apartment	20
Not enough steam	19
Urine, garbage smells in building halls	19
Not enough hot water	18
Faulty plumbing	17
Rotting building staircase	16
Little light in apartment	16
Little ventilation in apartment	16
Obscenities written on building hall walls	15
Little light in building halls and stairwells	15
Holes in building floors or walls	12

[a] Remaining categories of negative conditions are: exposed wiring, other building hazards, and other dwelling unit hazards; 3 percent of the households had each of those negative conditions.

causal relationship between poverty and foster care. It is merely intended to document the initial hypothesis of this chapter—that families with children in care have much in common with other families who are at minimum levels of living.

HOUSEHOLD COMPOSITION. In any consideration of the economically disadvantaged family, household composition is a critical area of study. Membership in a female-headed household has been noted in national studies to be strongly linked with the risk of poverty. Orshansky states:

> . . . the economic deprivation associated with a father's absence was more common than it used to be: in 1966 it was one in three of all poor children who did not have a father, not one in four as was the case in 1959. To make matters worse, the poverty rate among children in families headed by a woman was now 4½ times as high as in families headed by a man, whereas in 1959 it was 3⅓ times as high.[14]

As shown in Table II.9, mothers were heads of households in 37 percent of the families from which study children were placed, with no adult male residing in the home. Here again, the study group, although reflecting the pattern of families in poverty, was unlike the overall population. The Population Health Survey [15] estimated that in 1966 only about 15 percent of all families in New York City had female heads.

Not only were a large proportion of the sample children placed from mother-headed households, but prior to entering foster care 21 percent of the children were living with relatives other than their parents or with non-relatives. In addition, 12 percent of the study children had never experienced home life with their own parents at all, having been placed directly from the hospitals in which they were born. Three-quarters of the children, therefore, were not experi-

14. Orshansky, "The Shape of Poverty in 1966," p. 23.
15. Kogan, *Estimates of Population Characteristics*, p. 6.

TABLE II.9

Composition of Households of Study Children
Just Prior to Placement (N = 533)

	Percent distribution
Both natural parents	11
Natural mother, no male adult in home	37
Natural mother, male adult other than natural father in home	3
Natural father, no female adult in home	10[a]
Natural father, female adult other than natural mother in home	5
Grandparent, parents not in home	8
Other relative, neither parent nor grandparent in home	7
Non-relative, no relative in home	6
Hospital or institution	12
Not ascertainable	1
Total	*100*

[a] In almost all these cases the mother had usually been in the home, but just prior to placement she was hospitalized, institutionalized, or deceased.

encing either the normal child-father or the normal parent-child relationship. The number of single-parent, father-headed households just prior to placement was also significant.

DEMOGRAPHIC FACTORS. As an aid in understanding family background, information was obtained about the religion, age, birthplace, education, and work experience of all parents of the study children. Data were also collected about the marital status and childhood background of the

297 mothers and 137 fathers who were interviewed. In addition, some facts about the children's maternal grandparents were gathered.

Religion. The religious affiliation of more than half of the study families, 58 percent, was Catholic. Protestant families comprised 35 percent of the study group, and Jewish families, 7 percent. The white and Puerto Rican groups were primarily Catholic, whereas the black group was predominantly Protestant.

TABLE II.10

Percent Distribution of Study Families
by Religion and Ethnic Group
(N = 390)

		Ethnic group		
Religion	Total	White	Black	Puerto Rican
Catholic	58	16	13	29
Protestant	35	2	30	3
Jewish	7	6	1	—
Total	100	24	44	32

Age. Most of the mothers and fathers of children in the study were in their twenties or thirties when their children entered care. Few were teenagers and only about one-fifth were 40 years old or more. The men were generally slightly older than the women. The median age for fathers of placed children was 34 years, and for mothers, 31 years. Since the sample did not include children over 12 years of age, it is understandable that the parents would be relatively young. There were differences in age according to ethnic group and religion. One-half of the black women

36

TABLE II.11

Age of Mothers and Fathers of Study Children

Age	Percent distribution of mothers (N = 390)	Percent distribution of fathers (N = 390)
Less than 20 years	5	1
20 to 29 years	39	23
30 to 39 years	35	35
40 or more	18	23
Not ascertainable	3	18
Total	100	100

were under 30 years of age, whereas almost two-thirds of the white women were 30 years or older. Jewish mothers were much the oldest group, 85 percent being 30 years or older.

Birthplace. A large proportion of the parents had been born outside of New York City, principally in Puerto Rico or in the South. Only one-quarter of the fathers and one-third of the mothers reported New York City as their birthplace. One-fifth of both the men and the women had been born in the South and one-quarter in Puerto Rico. The great majority, 88 percent, of Puerto Rican mothers had been born in Puerto Rico, and only ten percent had been born in New York City. Half of the black mothers were Southern born, whereas only one-third were born in New York City. A higher proportion of black Protestant mothers (58 percent) had been born in the South than black Catholic mothers (35 percent). Almost half of the black Catholic women were born in New York City, but this was

37

TABLE II.12

Birthplace of Mothers and Fathers of Study Children

Birthplace	Percent distribution of mothers (N = 390)	Percent distribution of fathers (N = 390)
New York City	35	26
Southern United States	23	21
Puerto Rico	28	28
Other United States	5	5
Outside United States	6	7
Not ascertainable	3	13
Total	100	100

true for less than a third of the black Protestant mothers. A substantial majority of white mothers (two-thirds) reported New York City as their birthplace.

Education. The majority of the parents in the study had not completed the tenth grade in school. Available data indicated the median number of years of education completed by mothers was 9.4 years, and by fathers 9.8 years. This is considerably below the 1967 nationwide average of 12.0 years.[16] White mothers as a group had the most years of education and Puerto Rican mothers the least. Only 8 percent of the Puerto Rican women, 26 percent of the black women, and 43 percent of the white women were high school graduates.

Work experience. Forty percent of the study mothers had

16. U.S. Bureau of the Census, *Statistical Abstract of the U.S.: 1968* (89th ed., Washington, D.C.), Table No. 156, p. 110.

never worked. Among those mothers who had worked, clerical and operative occupations predominated. On the other hand, very few of the fathers (5 percent) about whom data were available had never worked. The men primarily held operative, service, and clerical jobs, and few were either professionals or laborers. Black and Puerto Rican mothers were more likely to have worked than white mothers. The white mothers with work experience were primarily clerks. Puerto Rican working women were mainly operatives. No one occupation predominated among working black mothers, who were, in equal numbers, service workers, operatives, or private household workers.

Marital status. It was possible to obtain direct information about the marital status of the study children's parents from only the 297 mothers and 137 fathers who themselves were interviewed, since it was considered inappropriate to

TABLE II.13

Marital Status of Interviewed Mothers and Fathers

Marital status	Percent distribution of mothers (N = 297)	Percent distribution of fathers (N = 137)
Single	36	17
Divorced	7	6
Widowed	3	7
Married	54	69
Living with spouse	18	37
Not living with spouse	36	32
Not ascertainable	—	1
Total	*100*	*100*

make such inquiries of informants. Of the parent respondents, somewhat over one-third of the women were single and had never been married, and an additional 10 percent were divorced or widowed. The remaining women (54 percent) were married but most of them were not living with their spouses. Fewer interviewed men than women were single, and more of the men were married and living with their wives (not necessarily the women who were the mothers of the study children). It should be noted that the sample of mothers interviewed is more representative of all the study families than is the father sample, since the most pathological and inaccessible of the latter group were not included in the father interview.[17]

Childhood background of parents. As with marital status, accurate data on childhood experiences of the mothers and fathers of the study children were available only for the interviewed parents. Only about half of the interviewed mothers, but 70 percent of the interviewed fathers, had been raised by both their natural parents. Those men and women who had not grown up in intact homes were raised by either their own mothers only or by a relative. Fifteen percent of the women and 10 percent of the men themselves experienced foster care placement as children. Three percent of both the men and the women spent all or most of their childhood in foster care.

The placed children's maternal grandparents. Some information was obtained about the birthplace, education, and occupation of the maternal grandparents of the sample children. The data obtained are not complete, since the respondents in many cases did not know these facts. The in-

17. See discussion of study sample in Chapter 1.

formation collected, however, does shed considerable light on generational differences between the parents and maternal grandparents of the study children.

Although it has been noted that only about one-third of parents of study children were native New Yorkers, the proportion drops even lower in the previous generation. More than twice as many parents as grandparents were born in New York City. Almost all of the grandmothers and grandfathers were born in the South, in Puerto Rico, or in Europe.

At least half of the older generation had no schooling at all or only a grade-school education. Fewer of the grandparents than the parents went to high school, but, unlike the parents, if the grandparents did go they tended to finish and to graduate with a high school diploma.

Relatively more mothers of sample children had worked than had their grandmothers. Among those women who had worked, the grandmothers were more likely to have been private household workers, somewhat less likely to have been clerical workers, and equally likely as the mothers to have been operatives.

The children's grandfathers were most commonly laborers, craftsmen, or operatives, whereas their fathers tended to be operatives, service, or clerical workers. Considerably more grandfathers than fathers were laborers, but this was also true for professional and managerial jobs.

In comparing the two generations with regard to education and occupation, the older generation is more U-shaped in distribution, appearing at both extremes, whereas the younger generation tends to be bell-shaped in the middle of the range. The grandparents tended to have either no education or very little, or, on the other hand, to have graduated from high school. The parents, in contrast, tended to enter but not to graduate from high school. The grandfathers were more likely than the fathers to be either laborers, or professionals or managers. The fathers tended to be in more middle-level occupations, such as service and clerical jobs.

RESPONDENT'S KNOWLEDGE OF FACTS ABOUT FATHERS. In the findings on age, birthplace, educational attainment, and occupation of parents of placed children, information about fathers was not ascertainable for from 13 to 35 percent of the cases, depending on the particular variable. In a large number of instances the family respondent (in most cases the natural mother) did not know pertinent facts about the father. There were substantial differences among

TABLE II.14

Respondents Who Did Not Know Specified Fact
about Child's Father, by Ethnic Group

		Percent of respondents in ethnic group		
Demographic fact	Total (N = 390)	White (N = 94)	Black (N = 171)	Puerto Rican (N = 125)
Age of child's father	18	6	35	6
Birthplace of child's father	13	2	24	5
Educational attainment of child's father	35	19	44	35
Occupation of child's father	26	12	35	32

ethnic groups with regard to lack of such information. Black mothers reported the least: 35 percent of them said they did not know the father's age or occupation, 44 percent did not know his education, and 24 percent did not know his birthplace. For Puerto Rican respondents, age and birthplace were well known but education and occupation were not known by approximately one-third of the mothers.

SOCIOECONOMIC INDEX

In order to determine whether socioeconomic circumstances are related to other family characteristics, such as attitudes, feelings, and aspirations, it was necessary to develop a single quantitative measure which could be crosstabulated and correlated with other relevant variables. An index incorporating several characteristics was developed, with special attention being given to the particular nature of the study population. As the data have shown, a large proportion of the study families were living in deprived economic circumstances. The majority of families comprised mother-headed households, without a father in the home. Many of the women had never worked, or had negligible work histories and therefore no established occupations. In addition, in almost half of the cases public assistance was the main source of support. Widely used indexes for measuring socioeconomic conditions—for example, Warner's index of status characteristics [18] or the Hollings-

18. W. Lloyd Warner, *Social Class in America* (New York, Harper Brothers, 1960. First published in 1949 by Science Research Associates, Inc., Chicago.)

head and Redlich index of social position [19]—include variables such as amount of income and occupation, which are not relevant for this study group. As a consequence it was decided not to use the conventional socioeconomic indexes but to develop a new measure.

The socioeconomic level of the study families was relatively homogeneous when measured against the range of the general population. When it was examined internally, however, in terms of its own range and distribution, meaningful differences existed within the study group. An index which would reflect the spread between extremes of the relevant variables would highlight those differences and make comparisons possible in terms of other important variables in the study.

In the construction of the index the components included in most conventional socioeconomic indexes, e.g., means of support, education, and housing, were utilized, but the specific variables selected to represent those components were related to the special circumstances of the sample.[20] The following criteria were utilized:

1. To reflect the means by which a family supports itself, "main source of support," rather than income, was used. This differentiated among earned income, benefits, and welfare payments, and reflected the

19. A. B. Hollingshead and F. Redlich, *Social Class and Mental Illness* (New York, John Wiley, 1959).
20. For examples of the problems inherent in the construction of socioeconomic indexes for groups living in poor economic circumstances, see Mark Golden and Beverly Birns, "Social Class and Cognitive Development in Infancy," *Merrill-Palmer Quarterly*, 14, No. 12 (April 1968), pp. 139–49; and Patricia Coursey, Gertrude Leyendecker and Else Siegle, "A Socioeconomic Survey of Family Agency Clients," *Social Casework*, June 1965, pp. 331–38.

44

higher status traditionally given by society to self-supporting members (within the lower and middle class). Families supported primarily by salaries were then ranked according to amount of income, whereas families supported mainly by public assistance were differentiated by the length of time they had received public aid, as an indicator of chronicity of dependency.

2. To reflect the educational attainment of the household, the highest grade completed by any member of the household was utilized. Thus all adults to whom the child was exposed at home, rather than only natural parents, were considered to be potential influences in the child's social environment.

To reflect the quality of the area of residence of the family, two measures were used: [21]

3. "income rank" of the neighborhood in which the family lived relative to all New York City neighborhoods, and

4. "juvenile delinquency rank" of the neighborhood in which the family lived relative to all New York City neighborhoods.

5. To reflect the quality of the family's housing, the number of "negative housing conditions" existing in the home and dwelling (from a list of 21) was used.

The five-variable index thus constructed differentiates within the sample itself and highlights important distinc-

21. Jenkins, *Comparative Recreation Needs,* pp. 33–37.

tions in socioeconomic circumstances among the study families.

The data for each variable in the index pertain in time to the situation which existed just prior to placement of each child. One complicating factor in data collection was identifying the appropriate household for which the socioeconomic index should be computed. In only a minority of cases did the children, mothers, and fathers occupy the same premises just prior to the placement. Very often children were either with one or the other parent or with a relative or other child-caring person. Since no assumptions could be made before the facts were known about whether such different households were of relatively the same or of different socioeconomic levels, data were collected separately for households of children, of mothers, and of fathers, and the data were found to be different where they lived apart. Socioeconomic index scores were therefore assigned separately to children, mothers, and fathers, and three distributions on each scaled variable were obtained, as well as three composite indexes. This procedure allowed for comparison of the household situations and for use of the appropriate index depending on context, i.e., mother, father, or child.[22]

The development of the index is described in consider-

22. It should be noted that each of the three indexes relates to a different sample size. Although 390 families participated in the field study, only 297 mothers and 137 fathers were interviewed. In 61 cases the children were hospitalized or institutionalized just prior to the time of placement. This was also true for 57 of the interviewed mothers and 8 of the interviewed fathers. For these cases, no household data were obtained, and the resultant sample size for socioeconomic circumstances was reduced to 329 for child households, 240 for mothers, and 129 for fathers.

able detail in the Appendix. The procedures used have research implications for studies incorporating comparable variables—poverty, welfare status, low educational levels, and depressed economic conditions. The Appendix discusses the rationale for inclusion of each of the five variables in the socioeconomic index. The scaling procedures, weighting decisions, and standardization techniques utilized in the index construction are reported. Frequency distributions which compare mothers', fathers', and children's households on each of the five variables are incorporated in the Appendix tables. In addition, intercorrelations of the component variables are given for the children's households.

Once the computed index values were derived, each of the families was placed in a category of "high," "middle," or "low" according to the score achieved. Allocation of families was governed by a decision to place exactly one-third of the total sample in each category. Data have already been presented earlier in this chapter which show that the overall sample lived in deprived socioeconomic circumstances, when compared with the population as a whole. The study index is primarily useful, therefore, in differentiating within the study sample, and this was the rationale for spreading the scores in this manner.

SOCIOECONOMIC LEVEL BY ETHNIC AND RELIGIOUS GROUP. Differences in the distributions of socioeconomic levels were found to occur among the several ethnic and religious groups in the study. There were significantly different percentages of white, black, and Puerto Ricans in the three socioeconomic groups. White children (72 percent), white mothers (70 percent), and white fathers (58 percent) were most likely to come from households with high socioeconomic indexes. Black children, black mothers, and black fathers were fairly evenly divided among the three levels, with the middle predominating slightly. Puerto Rican children (49 percent), Puerto Rican mothers (57 percent), and Puerto Rican fathers (62 percent) came from homes with scores in the low range. The differences of socioeconomic level among ethnic groups proved to be statistically significant, as seen in Table II.15.

Significant differences in socioeconomic level were also found among religious groups. Catholics and Protestants tended to come from homes of middle or low socioeconomic circumstances, with a larger proportion of Catholics in the low category. Jewish children and their parents came primarily from homes in the high socioeconomic category, as seen in Table II.16.

When separate analysis was made of the socioeconomic levels of religious groupings within ethnic categories, one interesting trend was noted. This was seen in the children's households, where the sample was large enough for reliable analysis. In the black group, those who were Catholic, the minority religion, tended to live in households with higher socioeconomic circumstances than did those who were Protestant, the religion of the majority of blacks. A comparable phenomenon was seen in reverse among the Puerto Ricans, where the minority religious group, in this case the Protestants, also tended to have a higher level of living than did the majority, who were Catholics. Although the number of cases in each category is too small for generalization, there is a persistent tendency for the minority religious group within each ethnic classification to show distinct characteristics. This is a line of analysis interesting to pur-

TABLE II.15

Socioeconomic Level by Ethnic Group of Child, Mother, and Father

*Percent distribution
of household, by ethnic group*

CHILD[a]

Socioeconomic level	Total ($N = 329$)	White ($N = 74$)	Black ($N = 141$)	Puerto Rican ($N = 114$)
High	33	72	26	18
Middle	34	23	38	33
Low	33	5	36	49
Total	*100*	*100*	*100*	*100*

MOTHER[b]

	Total ($N = 240$)	White ($N = 60$)	Black ($N = 106$)	Puerto Rican ($N = 74$)
High	33	70	29	9
Middle	34	27	37	34
Low	33	3	34	57
Total	*100*	*100*	*100*	*100*

FATHER[c]

	Total ($N = 129$)	White ($N = 43$)	Black ($N = 44$)	Puerto Rican ($N = 42$)
High	33	58	32	12
Middle	34	23	48	26
Low	33	19	20	62
Total	*100*	*100*	*100*	*100*

[a] $\chi^2 = 72.45$; $P \leq .001$; $df = 4$
[b] $\chi^2 = 54.16$; $P \leq .001$; $df = 4$
[c] $\chi^2 = 33.43$; $P \leq .001$; $df = 4$

49

TABLE II.16

Socioeconomic Level by Religious Group
of Child, Mother, and Father

Percent distribution
of household, by religion

CHILD[a]

Socio-economic level	Total (N = 329)	Catholic (N = 194)	Protestant (N = 113)	Jewish (N = 22)
High	33	30	27	95
Middle	34	34	37	5
Low	33	36	36	—
Total	100	100	100	100

MOTHER[b]

	Total (N = 240)	Catholic (N = 131)	Protestant (N = 91)	Jewish (N = 18)
High	33	28	29	89
Middle	34	32	40	11
Low	33	40	31	—
Total	100	100	100	100

FATHER[c]

	Total (N = 129)	Catholic (N = 71)	Protestant (N = 36)	Jewish (N = 14)	Other (N = 8)
High	33	25	33	79	38
Middle	34	30	45	14	38
Low	33	45	22	7	24
Total	100	100	100	100	100

[a] $\chi^2 = 41.34$; $P \leq .001$; $df = 4$
[b] $\chi^2 = 35.54$; $P \leq .001$; $df = 4$
[c] $\chi^2 = 19.51$; $P \leq .01$; $df = 6$

sue, particularly in terms of exploring a hypothesis related to behavior of persons who are affiliated with minority religions within their own ethnic grouping.

This chapter, with its detailed review of family characteristics and circumstances, has served to document the range of variables that are associated with the poverty syndrome characteristic of most of the families in this study. Low income, welfare status, poor housing and depressed neighborhoods, single-parent and female-headed households, low educational levels, minimal or limited work history, migration from place of birth, illegitimacy, minority group membership—one or more of these are characteristic of the majority of families with children in foster care.

CHAPTER THREE

Placement of Children

FAMILY characteristics and socioeconomic circumstances of the study sample largely parallel those of the urban poverty population. There was scarcely a family who did not have multiple problems and numerous needs. There is, however, one unique variable which is characteristic of the study families—they all had children placed in foster care in 1966.

Through intensive review of case situations, it was possible to delineate a main reason for each placement. This specification of main reasons was important not only for descriptive purposes but also because reasons for placement were significantly related to other critical variables and were often predictive of the child's career in foster care.

Because of the multiplicity of problems in the study families, the main reason for placement was hard to identify. One way was to ask the following question: "What factor in this situation, if absent, would have meant that the child would probably not have entered care?" Such an approach, although seemingly negative, is a useful screening device, since the main reason for placement is not necessarily identical with the major social problem faced by a family. Thus, one family may face a terminal illness of the mother and not place a child because a relative can assume responsibility. In another family, particularly in a one-parent household, a relatively minor but incapacitating illness of the mother can be devastating, particularly if there are young children, and placement may be the only answer. Thus, it is not the seriousness or urgency of the family problem per se which is the main stimulus for placement, but rather its effect on the living situation of the children. The main reason for placement, therefore, reflects the way in which the social problem is related to problems of child care.

Criteria utilized to classify reasons for placement in the present study are based in part on established categories employed in the child welfare field by intake workers responsible for making decisions about entry into care. Those categories were amplified and extended on the basis of the research literature, in particular the study by Jenkins and Sauber, *Paths to Child Placement,* in which the year preceding entry into care was studied intensively for 891 children.[1] In addition, case material and reasons given by respondents to the social work interviewers in the present study were incorporated into the classification system. Numerous specific reasons for placement were used in the original coding procedures of the study, but these categories were ultimately reduced to a workable group of eight. These eight categories, as well as the number and percent

1. Shirley Jenkins and Mignon Sauber, *Paths to Child Placement, Family Situations Prior to Foster Care* (Community Council of Greater New York, 1966), pp. 63–66.

distribution of families in each category, are shown in Table III.1.

In the multiproblem family the task of identifying a single "main reason" for placement has many inherent risks. One of these is that such a classification does not contain mutually exclusive categories. The possible non-independencies among reasons are apparent. Thus, the emotionally disturbed child may come from a situation where there is family dysfunction, and the neglecting or abusing parent may also be mentally ill. Another difficulty is that the reasons noted represent different patterns of needs. Some reasons relate to individual incapacities of the child-caring person, such as mental or physical illness. Other reasons relate to inappropriate and antisocial behavior, such as neglect,

TABLE III.1

Distribution of Families According to
Reason for Placement

Reason for placement	Number of families	Percent distribution
Mental illness	86	22
Child behavior	63	16
Neglect or abuse	54	14
Physical illness	44	11
Unwillingness or inability to continue care	41	11
Family dysfunction	36	9
Unwillingness or inability to assume care	30	8
Abandonment or desertion	30	8
Other problems	6	1
Total	390	100

abuse, or abandonment. Still another category relates to the child's own problems of emotional disturbance. Finally, there is a set of reasons that relate to environmental conditions, emergency needs, and family dysfunction.

In some instances, the decision on the main reason for placement was made in terms of timing of events. Distinctions frequently had to be made between an emergency need and basic problems of family functioning. A specific example is the case of an ill mother who left her child with a neighbor or a relative when she went to a hospital for a brief stay. A prolongation of the hospitalization may have meant that the surrogate was no longer willing or able to care for the child, and placement ensued. In such a case, a decision would have to be made as to whether the main reason for placement was the mother's illness or the substitute's inability or unwillingness to continue care. The length of time of substitute care could become an important criterion in deciding on the appropriate reason for placement.

Further complications occur in defining a main reason for placement because of differences in perception of the case situation on the part of the mother, the agency worker, and the research interviewer. These differences are particularly apparent in situations involving neglect or abuse. There were few disagreements among the parties when a clear-cut case of physical illness was present. Differences in perception and consequent judgment were reconciled by making the "main reason" for placement the combined product of parental judgment, case record information, caseworker judgment, and social work interviewer designation. The research staff reviewed the data from all these sources, and two senior staff members made independent judgments of the main reason for placement on each case.

If the two judges disagreed as to the main reason, the opinion of a third staff member was obtained and a final decision was arrived at by consensus after consideration by all three judges.

Thus the "main reason for placement," as used in the present study, involves a careful balancing of all known relevant factors. The procedure described, which incorporated consideration of a range of factors, was undertaken to avoid a hasty or mechanical designation of reason for placement which would have been based on partial knowledge from one point of view. High reliability among judges was not difficult to achieve, since strict rules for categories were established and followed. What these time-consuming procedures, using material from different sources, primarily sought to accomplish was to improve validity in the sense of correspondence of the designated "main reason" with the actual reality of the case.

Even though the reason for placement given by the respondent to the interviewer was considered in arriving at the staff decision on main reason for placement, there were differences between staff judgment and respondent reason in 37 percent of the cases, with agreement in 63 percent. The extent of disagreement differed widely according to category. These disparities are shown in Table III.2, which indicates extent of disagreement, by reason for placement, between staff judgment and respondent designation of main reason.

For cases in which there were differences between respondents and staff, the respondents were generally more likely to note a reason for placement less critical of the child-caring person. When the staff judged the placement to be primarily due to neglect or abuse, those respondents who

TABLE III.2

Disagreement between Staff Judgment and Respondent
Designation of Reason for Placement

Reason for placement	Percent in category disagreeing with staff judgment[a]
Mental illness	31
Child behavior	30
Neglect or abuse	61
Physical illness	14
Unwillingness or inability to continue care	56
Family dysfunction	31
Unwillingness or inability to assume care	13
Abandonment or desertion	53
Total	37

[a] The percentage was computed for each category by dividing the number of respondents disagreeing with the staff judgment for their case by the number of cases in that category as determined by staff judgment.

did not agree most frequently reported that the placement had been precipitated by the child's behavior or that the placement had been forced by authorities against the parent's will. In cases where the staff judged the placement to be due to the unwillingness or inability of the child-caring person to continue care, disagreeing respondents most frequently stated that the placement occurred because of the child's behavior. And where staff judgments indicated placement was due to abandonment or desertion, disagreeing respondents most frequently stated that placement had occurred because the child-caring person was unwilling or unable to continue care.

In considering the categories under reason for placement it should be noted that the distribution of reasons is inevitably related to the nature of the sample and the procedures for selection. Several criteria were applied in determining the sample. One such criterion was that the child must have been in foster care for the first time. Another was age. All the children were under 13 years at the time of placement. A third was time in care. Children entered the sample only after they had remained in care for at least 90 days. Thus the "reasons for placement" refer to subteenage children who were placed in what is known in the field as long-term care, i.e., care extending for a three-month period or longer.

The way in which different sampling criteria can affect outcome can be seen by comparing percentage distribution of cases among categories in the present study with those in *Paths to Child Placement,* in which all placements were also initial.[2] In that study children from the ages of 6 months to 18 years were included, and they had to remain in care for only one day to become part of the study sample. Thus babies under 6 months were excluded, and the large group of unwed mothers who were unwilling or unable to assume care of their babies was thereby eliminated. The teenagers from 13 to 18 years were included, as were cases involving temporary care. For that sample, defined in those more inclusive terms, physical illness of the mother was the main reason for placement in 29 percent of the families, of which 8 percent were confinement cases. Since in the present study a child had to be in care a minimum of 90 days, instances of confinement and short-term illness were not included in this study. It is interesting that the percentages of each sample placed because of child personality

2. *Ibid.,* p. 64.

or emotional problems were almost identical; 17 percent in *Paths to Child Placement* and 16 percent for the present research. Mental illness was more prevalent as a reason for placement in the present study: 22 percent, as compared with 11 percent of cases in the study which included short-term placements. The main conclusion is that the inclusion of short-term or temporary care situations tends to give more emphasis to physical illness of the mother as a primary reason for placement rather than to mental illness. Thus the nature of the sample must always be considered when analysis or classification of the total group is reported.

REASONS FOR PLACEMENT:
CASE MATERIAL

Data on numbers in care and main reasons for placement provide a frame of reference for analytic study of the population with children in foster care. To achieve a deeper understanding of the actual life situations of these families and the complicated problems which give rise to placement, it is useful to look behind each statistical category to the case material, which was based on verbatim reports of field visits with mothers, fathers, or relatives of children in foster care recorded in the home by social work interviewers. From these data the circumstances of families can be delineated and the specification of eight categories can be better understood. Each category incorporates a range of case situations, but cases within each category tend to be more like each other than like cases in other categories. The cases presented below were chosen to represent typical situations. Where a category incorporated two major subcategories, a case representing each is included. The material presented should not only illustrate the categories, but aid in comprehending some of the special problems inherent in each of them.

MENTAL ILLNESS. Two major situations were incorporated in the category of mental illness. The first comprised cases in which the child-caring person, typically the mother, was institutionalized (with psychiatric diagnosis) in a mental hospital. These constituted 62 of the 86 mental illness cases. In the remaining 24, there was no actual hospitalization in a mental institution, but the symptoms and reported experiences of the child-caring person or of the relative or informant gave evidence that the individual concerned was not functioning according to normal capacity. Symptoms and behavior might be just as severe as in cases where hospitalization occurred, but for one reason or another the individual did not enter an institution.

Reference will be made to three case situations: (1) a mother's report of her own hospitalization; (2) a father's report of a mother's institutionalization; and (3) a case where hospitalization did not occur.

405: Mental illness, hospitalization of single parent
Miss M. is a black, Catholic woman from the Virgin Islands. She is 29 years old and single. She has four children living with her, one boy and three girls, ranging in age from 6 years to 10 months. An older girl, age 11, is in the Virgin Islands with Miss M.'s maternal grandmother. All these children have different fathers. Miss M. has a 10th-grade education. She is unemployed and has been supported by public assistance for the past six years. Prior to that she worked on and off in a factory. The interviewer described Miss M. as a quiet-spoken young

woman obviously overwhelmed by the responsibility of caring for four young children and guilty over the placement situation.

Miss M. related the following events as the situation which resulted in the placement of her 2-year-old daughter. "I was sick—left her in a department store. I don't know—something told me to do it. The rest of the children were at home by themselves. Someone from the store then placed her. . . . I just ran off. . . . After I left her I went downtown—bought a Bible and went to church to pray about my problems. Came home late in the afternoon. O. [Miss M.'s 6-year-old son] had taken care of the other children. He asked for P. I told him I left her in the department store. Later my mother came. O. told her what had happened. My mother took the younger children home and made me call my public assistance worker. The next day I had to go to the hospital."

495: Mental illness, hospitalization of mother and placement by father

Mr. S. is a 37-year-old Puerto Rican described by the interviewer as very sensitive and very concerned about his children. He is separated from his wife, by whom he has two children, and has lived in a common-law relationship with Miss L. for several years. They have three children, a boy and two girls, ranging in age from 7 years to 4 months. Miss L.'s daughter of another father, age 11, is also in the home. Mr. S. has two years of high school education and is employed as a porter in a hospital.

Mr. S. stated that Miss L. had been emotionally ill for about two years prior to the time of placement and was finally hospitalized at a state mental institution. Mr. S. stayed at home to care for the children and the family began receiving public assistance. The Department of Social Services also provided a homemaker for a brief period. Mr. S. considered sending the children to his mother in Puerto Rico, but Miss L. opposed this idea. Mr. S. attempted to care for the children alone for a month following Miss L.'s hospitalization, but found the task beyond him. "I could not cope with them. I simply did not know how to cook for them or dress them right. They would get sick often." At this point Mr. S. went to the Department of Social Services for help, and the worker suggested placement. Both parents were against the idea at first, but Mr. S. reported that the worker convinced him that he should return to work and that he was "being very selfish" to want to keep the children.

219: Mental illness, no hospitalization

Mrs. T. is a 23-year-old white woman, with four boys under the age of 5. She was divorced from her husband after a separation of a year and a half. She states that she never really got along with Mr. T., a man twelve years her senior; that he was a cruel and brutal man who beat her and who would disappear after each pregnancy. Mrs. T. was born in New York City. She is a high school graduate and gives her occupation as housewife. At the time of placement the family was maintained by support payments from Mr. T., a floor manager in a department store, and the salary of Mr. M., Mrs. T.'s fiancé, who lives with the family. He is an instructor on an antipoverty program. Mrs. T. has a history of emotional difficulties and suicide attempts and is under a doctor's care.

Two months prior to placement, Mrs. T.'s situation worsened after the birth of a fifth child, a girl, who soon became severely ill with bronchial asthma. Mr. M. was the father of this child. Mrs. T. became very depressed and felt overwhelmed by her responsibilities. "I was just too nervous and sick to be able to care for all the children. It was all too much. . . . I felt I was going to drop dead or commit suicide." Mrs. T. felt that she would be able to manage with the oldest boy and the new baby at home if the other three children were placed. She was upset about the placement, but felt she had no alternative. "I did not want the children to leave me and be separated, but there was nothing I could do. I knew that if I did not do something, I would get real sick. Also, my doctor said that it would be best for me."

CHILD BEHAVIOR. The category of child behavior refers to situations in which there is clear evidence that placement was the result of certain characteristics, needs, or behavior of the child himself. Thus, this category has a different orientation than other categories, in that it does not relate to the child-caring capacity of the responsible adult or to the environmental circumstances of the family. Here the child is the principal actor on the scene. This is not to say that other problems do not exist in the family. When the child exhibits severe behavior difficulties there is often parental inadequacy, and when the family seeks to place the child, very often there is lack of parental capacity to cope with the problem. In these cases, however, when the critical question is asked about why placement occurred, the answer focuses primarily on the child himself.

Within this category there are two main subgroups. One is the group having psychiatrically diagnosed emotional problems or behavioral difficulties which commonly result in placement in a residential treatment center. Such diagnoses were reported in 44 of the 63 child behavior cases. The second group, comprising the 19 remaining cases, consists of the acting-out children who have shown behavioral difficulty in home, school, or community but who have not been professionally diagnosed as having emotional problems. In such cases placement tends to be in a regular foster care home or institution.

Although two subgroups have been described, it should be noted that clinically many of these children are similar and, in fact, like many others in the study sample.[3] Thus,

3. At the time of placement, only children who entered the so-called "foster care system" were included in the study sample. Thus, children

children of mentally ill mothers or of neglectful or abusing parents might very well have severe emotional problems. The difference is that they would have entered care primarily because of the parental difficulty rather than their own disturbance.

To illustrate the situations of the children classified in this category, two case examples are given. The first describes a youngster with a diagnosed emotional problem and the second refers to an undiagnosed but acting-out child.

204: Child behavior, diagnosed

The B.'s are an intact, white, Jewish family. Both parents are college graduates and have attended graduate school. Both are employed in a professional capacity. Mr. B., 43, is an engineer, and Mrs. B., 42, teaches school. They have two children, a girl, age 14, and a boy, age 11.

Ever since he was an infant H. had been having temper tantrums, but around the age of 5 his behavior began to worsen. Mrs. B. describes H. as "a very angry boy of strong temper—a very destructive child." School only made the situation worse —the child "suffered from school phobia, he just could not get to school. He found all kinds of reasons for not attending." He was also having severe temper tantrums, was very destructive, and "did not get along with anyone at home." The family then took H. to a private doctor and to several hospitals. One year prior to placement H. was hospitalized for three months at a hospital unit for emotionally disturbed children. When he returned home he continued to see his private doctor, but Mrs. B. states, "He did not change. We were having the same problems with him all the time. This house was just unbearable with him

---

who entered directly into state training schools or state mental hospitals were excluded. Also excluded were children with severe physical handicaps or severe mental retardation.

here." Three months prior to placement H. returned to the hospital where he remained until arrangements could be made to transfer him to a residential treatment center. Mrs. B. said that "All along the doctors had been recommending institutionalization." She gave as the main reason for placement "H.'s effect on the entire family as a unit. He was destroying the family."

218: Child behavior, undiagnosed

Mrs. P. describes her 10-year-old daughter A. as "a mixed-up child, always on the go." Mrs. P. is 28 years old, of Puerto Rican background but born in New York City. She has an 8th-grade education. At 14 she ran away with and married A.'s father, a Puerto Rican man six years her senior who was employed as a taxi driver. He deserted the family eight years later when A. was 6, leaving four children. Two out-of-wedlock children were subsequently born, so that at the time of A.'s placement there were six children in the family, three boys and three girls, ranging in age from 12 years to 1 month. Mrs. P. has never worked and the family has received public assistance since Mr. P.'s desertion. Mrs. P. also receives a small weekly contribution from the father of the youngest child.

Following her husband's desertion, Mrs. P. became too upset to care for the children and A. spent a year with a paternal grandmother. It was following this year that A.'s behavior problems became more serious. Mrs. P. states that Mr. P. had always been cruel and rejecting toward this child, and that he and his family "hated" her. By the age of 10 A. was having serious sexual problems. "A. gave me a lot of problems—it's so embarrassing even to talk about it. She's only 10, but she got involved with older boys and was having homosexual relationships with girls. . . . I decided to place her because she used to try sexual relations with her own brothers and sisters. She is tall and looks older than her years. She was always out—played hookey from school." Mrs. P. took the problem to her welfare worker, who referred the case to the Bureau of Child Welfare.

NEGLECT AND ABUSE. In those cases in which the main reason for placement is neglect and abuse, a judgment has been made about the deleterious quality of child care. These are cases which typically come to the attention of authorities either through complainants in the neighborhood, the Society for Prevention of Cruelty to Children, the police, or on occasion by self-referral on the part of abused children. Of the 54 neglect and abuse cases, 36 entered care under the sponsorship of the Family Court, with the remaining 18 being under the jurisdiction of the Department of Social Services. In almost all these cases it is noteworthy that the child-caring person denied responsibility for the situation, often placing blame for the problems on the child himself.

These cases can be subgrouped into neglecting families and abusive families, although on an overall basis the category refers to situations in which the health and welfare of the child are at risk. In the cases of severe neglect, this danger occurs because critical needs of the child are not being met. In the abuse cases, the danger occurs from active physical maltreatment of the child on the part of parent or guardian.

Once again, the differentiation between this and other categories should be emphasized. The child of the mentally or physically ill mother may also be neglected, but the parent's incapacity is the main reason for placement. In this neglect category, however, the family adult members remain in the household and in the community, typically showing little guilt or comprehension of their own actions with regard to their children. The child's needs, however, become so critical that he or she comes to the attention of the authorities in spite of the denial by the child-caring persons.

A case from the severe neglect group and one from the abuse group illustrate the kinds of situations defined herein.

089: Neglect

Miss G. is a 29-year-old Puerto Rican woman who has a 6th-grade education and speaks almost no English. She has done factory work, but the family has been supported by public assistance for the past seven years. Prior to placement, five of her six children, three boys and two girls ranging in age from 9 years to 6 months, lived with her in a four-room apartment. Miss G.'s sixth child, a boy of 8, has been hospitalized for over a year due to epilepsy and lead poisoning. The father of the five oldest children deserted the family four years prior to the date of placement. He was never legally married to Miss G. She says of him, "Their father was lazy. He would not work. He hit me when I told him to get himself a job. Then I took him to Court. So he left the house." Miss G. is hoping to marry the father of the youngest baby when he obtains a divorce from his present wife. He is a 23-year-old Puerto Rican man who is employed, but she reports he earns only $47 per week.

Miss G. states that the two oldest children entered placement because they were having difficulties in school, and an investigator from the school told the Court that Miss G. could not provide for her children and was neglecting them. Miss G. opposed the placement and felt that it was unneccesary. The three younger children were not placed because Miss G. told the Court that she could care for them. Miss G. gave the following account of the events leading up to the placement of her children. About three months prior to the date of placement, ". . . Mr. M. from the school came to visit unannounced. He found the home all messed up. I guess that is how the house is all the time. You see, I have no furniture. I have no money to buy things for the house or clothes for the children. But no matter how messed up the house looks, I love my children.

. . . Later Mr. M. informed the Court that I could not provide for the children. He said I was neglecting them. O. [a 9-year-old girl] was not going to school. A. [a 6-year-old boy] would fall asleep in class. I don't know why, he slept well at home. Maybe the girl was not attending every day, but I don't think I neglected them. Well, the Court believed everything Mr. M. said, and they took both children away."

[The social worker who interviewed Miss G. in her home three months after placement commented on the appearance of the children remaining in the home. The two boys were naked and the girl wore a torn little dress. He stated that the living room contained only three wooden chairs and the beds looked very old and broken with no coverings. From observation he questioned whether the children were getting the necessary care and whether household accommodations were adequate.]

151: Abuse

Miss B. is a 22-year-old black woman. She has two children, a girl of 2½ and a boy of 1 year. Her mother died when she was 8 years old, and she was raised by an uncle. The family lived in the southern United States. Miss B. is a high school graduate. She has occasionally done domestic work but has been supported by public assistance for the past three years. Miss B. never lived with the father of the older girl and doesn't think he knows he has a child. He is married to another woman. The father of the younger boy lives near the family and Miss B. is still friendly with him. Miss B.'s daughter was placed by Court order after being hospitalized for burns on her hands.

Miss B. states that ever since her daughter's birth she had "wanted to make an adult of her . . . I expected too much of her. I beat her a lot. The next door neighbors heard the child crying and said they would call the police the next time and they did. But I wasn't beating her. She was washing up—turned on the hot water and burned herself and screamed." Miss B. said that she felt "very, very bad" about the placement "because my uncle [who raised her] was so good to me. I felt that

I had been cruel to her. . . . I felt terrible and a failure as a parent." She did, however, feel that the placement was at least somewhat necessary "because I sometimes got carried away while beating her. If I had beaten her one more time I probably would have killed her." The younger boy remained in the home because "the neighbors felt I didn't treat him the same as I treated her."

PHYSICAL ILLNESS. This is a fairly straightforward category, in which the physical illness of the child-caring person is the essential reason the youngster enters foster placement. Since the sample includes only children in care for 90 days or more, it is apparent that the kinds of illnesses experienced must be of fairly long duration. Of the 44 families included the mother or child-caring person was hospitalized in 37 cases, and in another seven cases of serious physical illness hospitalization did not ensue. Two examples of physically ill mothers unable to care for their children are included as case illustrations, one hospitalized and one at home.

212: Physical illness, hospitalized

Miss C. is a 35-year-old unmarried Puerto Rican woman who suffers from arthritis. She has seven children, five girls and two boys, ranging in age from 14 years to 1 year. Miss C., who has a 3rd-grade education, has never worked, and the family has been supported by public assistance for the past eight years. Miss C. has no relatives or close friends in New York City.

About a week before the actual date of placement Miss C.'s arthritis became so severe that she could barely move. "I had to enter the hospital one night. I left the children alone. I was discharged the same night, but the next day I had to go in again. I didn't think I was going to have to stay, so I left the children alone with the oldest one [a 14-year-old girl] caring for them. She of course couldn't care for them herself once I had to stay in, so the grocer downstairs called the police and they placed the children." Six of the seven children went into placement and the oldest girl stayed with the family of the building's superintendent. Miss C. states, "I understand they first tried to find some lady but couldn't. Nobody could care for all six."

234: Physical illness, not hospitalized

Mr. and Mrs. B. are a young Puerto Rican couple with two small boys, ages 3 and 1. Mr. B. who is 23 years old and has an 11th-grade education, worked as a factory hand and supported the family until his hospitalization for tuberculosis four months prior to the date of placement. Mrs. B., age 20, with a 9th-grade education, began receiving public assistance and continued to care for the boys at home. But she was also ill with what she describes as "a lung infection, almost TB," and felt very weak. Her physical difficulties were increased by the fact that she had to walk up six flights of stairs with the children to reach her apartment. She sought help from relatives, but her husband's family were unable to help out and her own mother has four other children of her own to care for and had recently undergone a hernia operation.

Mrs. B. states that the social service worker at the hospital where she was an outpatient knew that Mrs. B. "couldn't attend to the children well, so she called welfare. . . . The doctor said I needed a lot of rest and the kids should be placed. . . . I felt sad, but what could I do? It was for their good and mine. . . . I had to get well and the doctors thought it was for the best, so I was resigned."

UNWILLINGNESS OR INABILITY TO CONTINUE CARE. The twofold reason, "unwilling" or "unable" to continue care has been utilized because of the difficulty of making an objective judgment as to which of these is in fact the more descriptive statement. In many cases the distinction in respondent reports between "unwillingness" and "inability" is a semantic one. Considering the problems with which the families had to cope, whether care ceases because of inability or unwillingness tends to depend on the extent of commitment to the child and the difficulties of the child care situation.

In several of these 41 cases, the child-caring person was someone other than the natural mother, and the cessation of care was a reaction to the fact that temporary care had been expected, but the extended period during which care was needed went beyond the capacity of the substitute. This often occurred despite positive attitudes toward the child and a real concern about his future. In such cases policy issues often arise regarding support for children who are not related to the child-caring person. Such an illustration is presented below.

246: Unwillingness or inability to continue care

Mrs. L. is a 34-year-old black woman with no children of her own. For the past two and one-half years she has cared for and supported L., a little girl who was abandoned by her mother when she was an infant, along with her four brothers and sisters. The child was raised by Mrs. L.'s grandmother, a neighbor, until her death, at which point Mrs. L. assumed care.

Six months prior to the time of placement, Mrs. L. separated from her husband and came to New York City from New Orleans, bringing L., age 8, with her. Mrs. L., who has an 11th-grade education, was able to find work in a factory, but her pay was low and she found it hard to support herself and the child. Mrs. L. gave the following as the reason for her decision to put the child into placement: "The mother of the child abandoned the children. We lived close by and my grandmother took L. Some other neighbors took the other children. My grandmother cared for L. until two and one-half years ago. When she died I decided to look after L. I came with her to New York, found a job, and supported her the best I could. Then I was laid off from work and could no longer support her. The welfare refused to give me help for her in my own home. When I began to work again my salary was only about $47 per week. I pay $25 per week for rent. I just could not manage . . . I was very confused. I just did not know what else to do. I could not support her. She also changed very much since we came here from New Orleans. She used to tell such lies. I was frightened. I spoke to the school about this. She was tested and the psychologist stated that she will need help. Ias sorry this happened."

UNWILLINGNESS OR INABILITY TO ASSUME CARE. In almost all cases where the main reason for placement is unwillingness or inability to assume care, the child was born out of wedlock, and the mother did not wish to assume the maternal role. Many of these babies were left in the hospital or placed directly following birth; others were in the care of the mother for a very brief period. The following case describes a typical situation of an unwed mother.

195: Unwillingness or inability to assume care

Miss R. is a 20-year-old black college student. The father of her 2-month-old daughter is a fellow student who is no longer concerned about Miss R. or her baby. He has never seen the child and Miss R. did not bother to tell him about her plans for placement because she "didn't think he would care one way or another." Miss R. left college after her sophomore year when she became pregnant and returned to New York City where she lived with her parents in a two-room apartment in a rooming house. Both of her parents are employed. Her father is a train operator and her mother works nights as a nurse's aide. They have a combined net income of $160 per week. Miss R. decided to place her baby so that she could complete her education and because there was no one else in the family who could care for her. The baby went into placement directly from the hospital of birth.

In discussing her reasons for placing the child, Miss R. said, "Both my mother and I had the idea of placing the child since there was no other way. I wanted to return to school. I feel completing my education is the most important thing at the present time. My mother could not care for the child since she is employed. . . . I was sad and at the same time glad that she would be cared for, and I would not have to give her up for adoption. I can look forward to having her with me in the future."

ABANDONMENT OR DESERTION. The abandonment or desertion situations were those in which the child-caring person, usually the mother, left the child or children with no indication of return. In some instances it is difficult to distinguish these from the neglect situations, but among the criteria for differentiation are difficulty of contacting the abandoning parent and lack of any kind of planning on her part for the child's future care or needs. There were 30 such cases in the study. The case illustration below describes a typical situation.

289: Abandonment or desertion

Mrs. M. is a 37-year-old white woman with a 7-year-old son. She is legally married to Mr. M., a Puerto Rican man, but has been separated from him since before the birth of their son. Mrs. M. is a high school graduate. She has never worked and the family has been supported by contributions from Mrs. M.'s mother, Mrs. P., who would give her daughter money for rent or food whenever it was needed. Mrs. P., age 60, is employed as a saleswoman in a large department store. She also supports her husband, Mr. P., who is 72 years old and retired. Mr. P. disowned his daughter because of her marriage to a Puerto Rican and has had nothing to do with her since that time. He is openly hostile toward his grandson.

Two weeks prior to the child's placement Mrs. M. left him at her parents' home. She had left the boy before, but had always returned for him within a day or two. When it became apparent that Mrs. M. was not returning for the child, the grandparents decided on placement because they were unable to care for him. Mrs. P. gave the following as the reason for placement. "My daughter brought the boy to my home. She left town and did not come back for him. My husband, who has not spoken to her since she married the Puerto Rican, returned the boy to our daughter's home and left him in the hall. A few hours later a neighbor brought him back stating that his mother had disappeared. We tried to take care of him; however, it was too much for us. I have to go to work and my husband is old and sick. . . . I thought it was the best thing for the child. It is not so bad to have the experience of an institution. My husband always states that he was brought up in an institution in France and he was treated very well. I was very relieved to know that the boy was in a good place and that he would be cared for."

FAMILY DYSFUNCTION. This has been used as a residual or umbrella-type category in which to place 36 personal or family situations which resulted in the child's entering foster care.

Among the subgroups in this category are 13 cases in which the child-caring person was arrested, 7 cases of extreme family conflict, and 14 cases where the child-caring person was considered to be incompetent due either to severe alcoholism, drug addiction, mental retardation, or inability to manage household affairs. As can be seen, these families represent only 9 percent of the overall study sample. For this 1966 cohort of placed children, therefore, it cannot be said that drug addiction or alcoholism was of great importance in contributing to placement of children. Nevertheless, it should be noted that this is not to say that these factors were not also involved in family situations where another primary reason such as abuse, mental illness, or abandonment was designated. The following case material is more specific in describing a family situation so classified.

156: Family dysfunction, alcoholism

Mr. and Mrs. L. are both alcoholics. They have one child, a girl of 6, who was born blind due to congenital cataracts and now sees only poorly with the help of thick glasses. Mr. L. is white, 54 years old, and a high school graduate. He has two adult children by a previous marriage. He is employed as a building superintendent and has been able to support his family. Mr. L. states that he has been an alcoholic since he was 15 years old. For the past ten years he has been a member of Alcoholics Anonymous and has been helped to stop drinking. For two years prior to placement he has had a heart condition. Mrs. L. is white, 45 years old. She was born in Ireland. Mrs. L. is a college graduate. She has never worked and has been drinking heavily for about five years.

At the time the child entered placement Mrs. L. had been hospitalized for alcoholism following a long drinking episode. Then Mr. L. suffered a heart attack and was also hospitalized. A friend from AA cared for the child for a week, but Mr. L. felt she was "a high strung person . . . not the type to care for children," and so he arranged for the child's placement until the parents could resume care.

FACTORS RELATED
TO PLACEMENT SITUATIONS

In the family interview, after determination of the respondents' perception of reason for placement, a series of questions were asked about the background of the placement situation. Data were sought on the following factors: timing of onset of main reason for placement; the initiator of the placement process; respondent judgment of the necessity for placement; alternative prior arrangements; preparation of children for entry into care; and who actually took the child to the agency setting. In addition, main reasons for placement as described in the eight major categories were analyzed in terms of various demographic variables such as ethnic group, religion, and socioeconomic level.

TIMING OF ONSET OF MAIN REASON. Following their statement of main reason for placement, respondents were asked, "When would you say that this problem first started?" The timing of the onset of the main problem, therefore, is related to the respondent's perception of main reason for placement, rather than to staff judgment. In 31 percent of the cases, the problem leading to placement was seen by respondents as having begun less than one month prior to the actual entry into foster care. In 24 percent of the families, the problem was reported as having begun from one to twelve months before placement, and in 26 percent of cases, the problem was reported as having existed for over one year. One out of every five family members interviewed (19 percent) was not able to estimate the timing of the onset of the problem.

Respondents who reported the main reason for foster care to be physical illness, unwillingness or inability to continue care, or abandonment or desertion tended to feel that the problem began less than a month before placement. When the reason reported was neglect or abuse, the problem was felt to have begun six months or less before placement. Nine months prior to placement was most frequently seen by the unwed mothers as the time when their difficulties began! The problems leading to placements due to child behavior were generally seen as having started more than a year before foster care. When mental illness of the child-caring person or family dysfunction were seen as the most important factor leading to placement reports of the timing of onset were bimodal. Such problems were reported either as having begun less than one month before placement or as being of long duration, more than a year.

INITIATORS OF PLACEMENT PROCESS. Problems leading to placement varied in their duration from sudden crises to long-term chronic situations. The idea of utilizing foster care as a way of handling these problems originated from various sources. Most frequently it was initially suggested by one or both parents of the placed child (36 percent of cases) or by another relative (14 percent). Official regulatory institutions or agencies or professional workers related to the police, the Society for the Prevention of Cruelty to Children, or the Family Court were next in frequency as being initiators of placement (12 percent of cases), followed by medical institutions or agencies, doctors, psychiatrists, and professional workers in clinics or hospitals (8 percent). Bureau of Public Assistance workers initiated placement in 8 percent of cases; school counselors in 6 percent; other social agencies or professionals in 5 percent; and the remaining cases were referred by friends or neighbors.

Associations were noted between who initiated placement and the main reasons for entry into care. Although there were a variety of initiators for almost every placement reason, some groupings of reasons and initiators occurred with markedly greater frequency than others, as shown in the following compilation relating initiator to placement reason.

PLACEMENT OF CHILDREN

Initiator	*Main Reason for Placement*
Parents	Mental illness of child-caring person
	Unwillingness or inability to assume care
	Child behavior
	Abandonment or desertion
	Family dysfunction
Relatives	Mental illness of child-caring person
	Physical illness of child-caring person
	Unwillingness or inability to continue care
Official regulatory agencies: (police, SPCC, Court)	Neglect or abuse
Medical settings	Child behavior
	Physical illness of child-caring person
	Unwillingness or inability to assume care
Bureau of Public Assistance	Mental illness of child-caring person
	Physical illness of child-caring person
	Abandonment or desertion
School counselors	Child behavior
Social agencies and professionals related to them	Mental illness of child-caring person
	Child behavior
Friends and neighbors	Physical illness of child-caring person
	Abandonment or desertion
	Family dysfunction

79

NECESSITY OF PLACEMENT. Each family member interviewed was asked the question, "Considering the circumstances, would you say that the placement of this child was (1) absolutely necessary, (2) very necessary, (3) somewhat necessary, or (4) not necessary at all?" In 40 percent of the cases, the placement was considered by the respondent to be absolutely necessary; in 21 percent, very necessary; in 16 percent, somewhat necessary; and in 22 percent, not necessary at all. One percent of the respondents were not able to make a judgement. In general, the higher the socio-economic status of the family from which the child was placed, the more likely was the family member to judge the placement as absolutely or very necessary. There were additional relationships discernible between judgment of the necessity of placement and several other variables, including main reason for placement and jurisdiction of the case at entry.

Placement was considered absolutely or very necessary by a family member in over three-quarters of the cases where the main reason was one of the following: child behavior; physical illness of the child-caring person; unwillingness or inability to assume care. In fewer than half of the placements due to abandonment or desertion or family dysfunction and in less than one-quarter of the cases of neglect or abuse was placement considered by respondents to be absolutely or very necessary.

JURISDICTION OF CASE. Children who entered foster care in 1966 in New York City did so under the jurisdiction of either the Bureau of Child Welfare of the Department of Social Services or the Family Court. Cases which entered under the jurisdiction of the Family Court usually represented instances of serious neglect or abuse of the child. In 19 percent of the study families placement occurred under Family Court auspices; for the remaining 81 percent the Bureau of Child Welfare had jurisdiction at the time of entry. In 61 percent of the Court cases, family members judged the placement to have been only somewhat or not at all necessary; whereas in 67 percent of the Bureau of Child Welfare cases, family members judged the placement to have been absolutely or very necessary.

Children placed from homes of low socioeconomic status were much more likely than children from middle- or higher-status homes to enter foster care under the jurisdiction of the Family Court. Twenty-six percent of the black children, 20 percent of the Puerto Rican children, and only 4 percent of the white children entered care under Court jurisdiction.

ALTERNATIVES TO PLACEMENT. In only one-third of the study cases did family members attempt to make alternative arrangements prior to placement so that the child would not have to enter foster care. Most frequently child care from relatives was sought, but attempts were also made to obtain services of homemakers, friends, and neighbors. Since all these children were eventually placed, none of these alternative arrangements actually worked out. Among the reasons given were the following: homemakers were not available; families were not able to pay for services of non-relatives; and relatives were unable to help because of the burdens of their own households or because of their own poor health.

Alternative arrangements to placement were more frequently attempted for children from the relatively higher socioeconomic group in the sample than for children of the middle- or lower-level households. Alternative care was most often sought when the reason for placement was either physical or mental illness of the child-caring person or abandonment or desertion. Alternatives were least often attempted when the placement was due to unwillingness or inability of the mother to assume care or neglect or abuse.

Interviewed family members indicated that an attempt was made to prepare the child for placement in only 44 percent of the cases. In 32 percent no one prepared the child in any way, and in the remaining 24 percent of cases the interviewed family member did not know if the child had been prepared or not. In most cases where the child was given no preparation, the reasons given were: the child was too young to understand; the child was placed from the hospital in which he was born; the placement was too abrupt for any form of preparation. Most of the children who were given some type of explanation were prepared either by their parents, by the person who was caring for them at home, or by a placement agency worker.

Each of the family members interviewed was asked, "Did anyone help you get ready for the child's going into placement away from home?" In only 32 percent of the cases did the family member indicate that he or she had been helped in any way. In most cases where such help had been forthcoming, a worker from a foster care agency was the person who had offered it. The higher the socioeconomic status of the family member, the more likely he or she was to have received some professional preparation for the placement. The families of white children were most likely and the families of black children were least likely to receive such preparation.

There remains the question of who actually took the child from his home to the agency setting in which he was to be placed. Most frequently—for one-third of the families—a worker from the Bureau of Child Welfare, the Bureau of Public Assistance, or the placement agency was the person who took the child into care. In one-quarter of the cases, one or both parents brought the child from home to the foster care agency. In about one in six cases, a policeman or a worker from the SPCC or the Family Court delivered the child to placement. In the remaining cases, the transporter of the child was either a relative other than the parents, a concerned non-relative, a worker from another type of social agency, or a community professional.

REASON FOR PLACEMENT BY DEMOGRAPHIC VARIABLES: ETHNIC GROUP, RELIGION, AND SOCIOECONOMIC LEVEL. There were substantial differences in the proportion of families from each ethnic and religious group whose children entered care for the various placement reasons. White families, for example, tended to place children in care because of the mental illness of the child-caring person or the child's behavior, but were less likely than families of other ethnic groups to have children in care for reasons of neglect or abuse or family dysfunction. The children of black families were more likely than the children of other families to be placed because of neglect or abuse, unwillingness or inability on the part of the mother to assume care, or family dysfunction. In comparison with the children of other ethnic groups, the black children were least likely to have been placed because of mental illness of the child-caring person.

TABLE III.3

Reason for Placement by Ethnic Group and Religion

Ethnic group and religion of child (Percent distribution)[a]

Reason for placement	Puerto Rican Catholic (N = 115)	White Catholic (N = 63)	Black Catholic (N = 49)	Black Protestant (N = 120)	Jewish (N = 27)
Mental illness	27	30	8	18	15
Child behavior	11	11	12	13	66
Neglect or abuse	16	8	23	17	—
Physical illness	15	13	10	9	4
Unwillingness or inability to continue care	13	8	14	6	11
Family dysfunction	8	6	17	12	4
Unwillingness or inability to assume care	1	13	12	13	—
Abandonment or desertion	9	8	2	10	—
Other	—	3	2	2	—
Total	100	100	100	100	100

[a] The six white Protestant and the ten Puerto Rican Protestant families are not included in this table because the numbers are too small for meaningful analysis.

Puerto Rican families were more likely than the others to have children in placement for reasons of physical illness of the child-caring person or because of unwillingness or inability to continue care. They were less likely to place children for reasons of child's behavior or unwillingness or inability on the part of the mother to assume care of the child.

Two-thirds of all Jewish children were placed because of child behavior. Apart from that, religion alone did not appear to be a significant factor in relation to the proportions of Catholic or Protestant children placed for specified reasons. Some distinctions, however, are apparent when religion within each ethnic group is studied separately (see Table III.3). Children of black Catholic families, for example, were more likely than children of Puerto Rican or white Catholic families to be placed for reasons of neglect or abuse or family dysfunction. On the other hand, they were less likely to be placed because of mental illness of the child-caring person or abandonment or desertion than were white or Puerto Rican Catholic children. Puerto Rican Catholic children were more likely than other Catholic youngsters to enter foster care because of the physical illness of the person who was caring for them and were less likely to enter placement because of the unwillingness or inability of their mothers to assume their care.

A comparison of reasons black Catholic and black Protestant children entered placement yields some striking differences. Black Protestant youngsters were far more likely than black Catholic youngsters to enter care because of abandonment or desertion or because of adult mental illness. The black Catholic child entered placement more frequently than the black Protestant child because of unwill-

TABLE III.4

Reason for Placement by Socioeconomic Level of Child Just Prior to Placement

	Total (N = 390)	Socioeconomic level (Percent distribution)				Placed from hospital or institution[a] (N = 61)
		High (N = 110)	Middle (N = 109)	Low (N = 110)		
Reason for placement						
Mental illness	22	23	24	26		12
Child behavior	16	26	7	15		16
Neglect or abuse	14	13	13	16		13
Physical illness	11	4	16	16		5
Unwillingness or inability to continue care	11	13	15	8		3
Family dysfunction	9	11	12	8		3
Unwillingness or inability to assume care	8	1	—	—		48
Abandonment or desertion	8	8	11	8		—
Other	1	1	2	3		—
Total	100	100	100	100		100

[a] No socioeconomic level determined for these cases.

ingness or inability of the adult to continue care, neglect or abuse, or family dysfunction.

Some differences are also apparent when the main reasons for placement are analyzed in terms of the various socioeconomic groups, as shown by Table III.4. Children placed from relatively higher socioeconomic levels in the study were more likely to enter placement because of their own behavior problems than children from either low- or middle-level homes but less likely to be placed because of the physical illness of the child-caring person.

Children placed directly from the hospital where they were born or from an institution were not assigned a socioeconomic status, since they were not placed directly from a home which could be evaluated. The largest proportion of such children, 48 percent, were born out of wedlock, and their mothers were unwilling or unable to assume their care.

This review of factors related to the placement situation points up the importance of the reason for placement as a critical variable in the study. There tends to be a general sameness in the family situations in terms of desperation, need for some way out of unworkable child care arrangements, and a typically unplanned approach geared to crisis situations. The particular patternings, however, vary according to the reason the child entered care. Interrelated with the placement reason are other important variables of a demographic nature, such as ethnic, religious, and socioeconomic status. No generalizations on the effect of these factors apply to every family in the study, but groupings of families do exist, and they have particular relevance for diagnostic procedures and service interventions.

EARLY CHILD CARE PATTERNS
AND SEPARATION EXPERIENCES

The immediate entry situations have been discussed, but child care patterns prior to the placement experience are also relevant to the study. Much of the theoretical interest in the foster care experience relates to the effect of separation and maternal deprivation on the children. There is substantial literature on the trauma experienced by children on such occasions. The inclusion of the criterion "first placement" in selecting the study sample was done deliberately to give fresh insight into the effects of the separation experience. The family interview data, however, and what was learned about family history introduce new material which indicates that, although the study sample was indeed experiencing initial formal placement through an agency, the majority of children had known substantial informal separations from their parents prior to official foster care.

Data on two aspects of these informal separations are presented here. The first aspect refers to the actual child-caring situation just prior to placement but often after the problem situation that led to placement was beginning to develop. The second aspect relates to the lifetime experiences of the children and their earlier separations from natural mother and natural father.

CHILD CARE PRIOR TO PLACEMENT. Although there were frequent temporary separations, approximately 77 percent of the sample children had been cared for primarily by their mothers throughout their childhood. Relatives other than the mother, typically the father or a grandparent, had raised approximately 11 percent of the children. An additional 8 percent had never had a home, having been placed in foster care directly from the hospital in which they were born.

Certain demographic variables in the research appear to be associated with different child care patterns. Fewer Puerto Rican infants (3 percent) than either white infants (10 percent) or black infants (11 percent) were placed directly from the hospital of birth. Related to this phenomenon is the fact that a larger proportion of Puerto Rican children (83 percent) were raised primarily by their mothers, as compared to white children (74 percent) or black children (75 percent). The natural mother was the usual child-caring person in 97 percent of Jewish families, as compared to 77 percent of Catholics and 75 percent of Protestants.

Although 77 percent of the children in the study were cared for during all or most of their lives by their natural mothers, due to crises just prior to placement only 51 percent were actually living with their mothers at that time (see Table III.5). The nature of preventive or at least pre-placement services necessarily has to be determined by whether parent(s) and child are living together or, if apart, just what arrangements have been made for the child's care.

Twelve percent of the children were hospitalized or institutionalized just prior to placement, as seen in Table III.5. In an additional 17 percent of cases the mother was hospitalized, institutionalized, or recently deceased. In most of these instances the child resided with a relative, usually his natural father. One out of every five children (20 percent of the cases) had been living in a separate household from his mother. The whereabouts of the mothers in most of these cases was not ascertainable. These children were usually

TABLE III.5

Whereabouts of Sample Child and Natural Mother
Just Prior to Placement (N = 533)

	Percent distribution	
Mother and child living together	51	
Child hospitalized or institutionalized	12	
Mother hospitalized or institutionalized, child with:	17	
Father		7
Grandparent		3
Other relative		3
Non-relative		3
Not ascertainable		1
Mother and child living in separate households, child with:	20	
Father		9
Grandparent		5
Other relative		3
Non-relative		3
Total	*100*	

living with relatives, in most instances their natural fathers or a grandparent. These data on the complicated preplacement situations show that there are often different answers to the questions, "Who constituted the child's family?" and "With whom was the child living?"

SEPARATIONS OF CHILD FROM NATURAL MOTHER OR NATURAL FATHER PRIOR TO PLACEMENT. There were relatively few children in the study who had not experienced some separation from their mothers or fathers prior to entering agency foster care. As seen in Table III.6, the majority of children had either had several lengthy separations from their parents or had never lived with them at all; 30 percent of the youngsters had never lived with their fathers, and 9 percent had never lived with their mothers. In addition, somewhat more than 40 percent of the children, although they had lived with at least one parent for most of their lives, had had several lengthy separations. Only 12 percent of the youngsters had never been separated from their fathers or had had only a few short separations of a week or less from them. No separations from the mother or very short ones had been the experience of only 32 percent of the children.

Black children were most likely to have never been sepa-

TABLE III.6

Separations of Children from Natural Mother
and Natural Father Prior to Placement (N = 533)

	Percent distribution of children separated from mother	Percent distribution of children separated from father
Parent never lived with child	9	30
Several lengthy separations of parent and child:	44	41
Cumulative time less than one year	30	13
Cumulative time more than one year	14	28
Parent never separated from child, or few short separations of one week or less	32	12
Not ascertainable	15	17
Total	*100*	*100*

rated from their mothers or to have had only a few short separations. They were also, however, most likely to have never lived with their fathers. All Jewish children in the study had lived with their mothers and fathers at some time prior to placement. They were, however, more likely to have had several lengthy separations from both parents than were Catholic or Protestant children.

The lower the socioeconomic level of the children, the greater chance they had of never having been separated from their mothers, and the reverse was also true. The higher the socioeconomic status of the child, the greater likelihood of his having had many lengthy separations from his mother. A different situation existed with regard to separations from the father. The lower the socioeconomic level of the youngster, the greater was the likelihood of his never having lived with his father at all.

AGE AND SEPARATION. It is well established that one of the most critical variables in analyzing the effects of child separation is the age of the child. For a sample which includes children from birth through age 12, each year obviously provides an added possibility for a separation experience. For this reason, an analysis of separations was done in terms of the child's age at placement, which was dichotomized into two main categories, children under six years old and children six or more. In cumulative time, the former category by and large had half the opportunities for separation than did the older children.

These data cannot be regarded as entirely reliable, since they are based on respondent recall. On the whole, however, it is likely that recall would tend to underestimate length of separations from children, rather than overestimate, since parents in reporting had a tendency to stress their involvement with the children rather than their disengagement from them. In some cases respondents were relatives or friends. Although these respondents might be able to report quite accurately on the situation just prior to placement, they could not be expected to have all the information on social history from birth. For this reason, a substantial number of cases were nonascertainable for this information. Within these limitations, however, it is of interest to compare separations from mother (Table III.7) and from father (Table III.8) in terms of the under six versus six or over dichotomy.

Several findings are apparent from a review of these data. Perhaps the most important is that these children, both younger and older, experienced a substantial amount of separation from both mothers and fathers before entering agency foster care. Only 13 percent of all children had never been separated from mothers, and 11 percent never separated from fathers. On the other hand, 9 percent of all children had never been with mothers and 30 percent had never been with fathers. Separations from mothers of one year and over were experienced by 14 percent of children, and similar separations from fathers by 28 percent of the children.

Young children in placement who are under six differ from those six or over in preplacement separation experiences. At the extremes, a higher proportion of the young children (19 percent) than of the older children (6 percent) have never been separated from their mothers. On the other hand, a higher proportion of the younger children (15 percent) than of the older children (1 percent) have never been with their mothers.

TABLE III.7

Children Separated from Mothers, by Duration of Separation and Age of Child

Duration of separation	All ages		Under six		Six or over	
	Number	Percent	Number	Percent	Number	Percent
Never separated	71	13	58	19	13	6
One day to one month	103	19	59	19	44	19
One month to one year	160	30	86	28	74	32
One year and over	76	14	15	5	61	26
Never with	47	9	45	15	2	1
Parent deceased	15	3	4	1	11	5
Not ascertainable	61	12	35	13	26	11
Total	533	100	302	100	231	100

TABLE III.8

Children Separated from Fathers, by Duration of Separation and Age of Child

Duration of separation	All ages		Under six		Six or over	
	Number	Percent	Number	Percent	Number	Percent
Never separated	60	11	40	13	20	9
One day to one month	4	1	3	1	1	—
One month to one year	70	13	41	14	29	13
One year and over	147	28	52	17	95	41
Never with	160	30	118	39	42	18
Parent deceased	10	2	1	—	9	4
Not ascertainable	82	15	47	16	35	15
Total	533	100	302	100	231	100

When the father data are reviewed, a somewhat different pattern is seen. Of the young children under six in placement, 39 percent have never been with their fathers. For the child at least six years old, the modal category of separation from fathers comprises 41 percent who have been apart from them for one year or longer.

In comparing separations from mothers and fathers in both age categories, the major differences are that mother separations tend to be briefer, falling most heavily in the one month to one year category in length, whereas father separations are longer for the older child, and there is a strong likelihood that the father of the young child has never been with him at all.

This exploration of the placement situation has focused on categorizing main reasons for entry into care, presenting case material to amplify family problems, relating a series of relevant variables to placement situations, and exploring data on early child care patterns and separation experiences. The plethora of family and child needs and the complicated and serious difficulties which have been documented lead to the conclusion that no simple solutions will readily be found to avoid foster care for the majority of children who enter placement, or even to ease the entry process. A strong case can be made for early intervention and preventive services to avoid the crises and perhaps placement as well for at least some of the children. Data on family situations indicate, however, that valid preventive work would have to reach beyond a narrow interpretation of child welfare and involve a broad spectrum of social, rehabilitative, and educational services.

CHAPTER FOUR

Feeling Dimensions and Referents in Filial Deprivation Experiences

FEELINGS experienced by parents on placement of their children in foster care run the gamut from sadness to relief, from shame to anger, from bitterness to thankfulness. These feelings and their referents were explored to help identify some aspects of the nature of filial deprivation, or the separation experiences of parents when their children enter care.

One aftermath of placement, the effect of maternal deprivation on children, has been a subject for major research investigation. The reciprocal aspect of the placement transaction, referred to here as filial deprivation, has not been similarly studied. In a society where the prevailing expectation is that parents will raise their own children, failure to do so, with placement of progeny in settings outside their own homes under social agency care, is likely to have serious consequences for the placing parents. How these feelings of separation from their children affect mothers and fathers and how their response patterns may be related to generalized attitudes of unworthiness or alienation are of interest and importance. Exploration of the concept of filial deprivation, and the identification of feelings expressed by parents when children enter foster care, has been a major focus of research in the present study.[1]

There are a number of reasons why clarification of the concept of filial deprivation is important to a better understanding of family separation. In terms of numbers affected, the problem is of major proportions. In 1967 there were 315,700 children living in foster families, group homes, or children's institutions in the United States. These figures report only formal public and voluntary agency data and do not include the myriad of informal, unreported arrangements for substitute care.[2] It is probable that the number of mothers and fathers who have at some time experienced separation from their children because of foster care placement would amount to several million. The fact that foster child placement also tends to involve a disproportionately high percentage of families who live in poverty, as well as families of minority groups, raises the further question of whether parental failure is interpreted by these groups as leading to social reprisals, such as abrogation of parental rights and loss of decision-making power over the

1. Some preliminary findings, which this chapter expands and amplifies, have been published in three articles by Shirley Jenkins: "Separation Experiences of Parents Whose Children Are in Foster Care," *Child Welfare*, June 1969, pp. 334–40; "Feeling Dimensions and Referents in Filial Deprivation Experiences," *American Journal of Orthopsychiatry* (digest of papers for Chicago conference), March 1968, pp. 256–57; "Filial Deprivation in Parents of Children in Foster Care," *Children*, January–February 1967, pp. 8–12.
2. U.S. Department of Health, Education, and Welfare, Social and Rehabilitation Service, *Child Welfare Statistics, 1967* (Children's Bureau Statistical Series 92, Washington, D.C., 1968).

raising of their own children. From the point of view of service, knowledge of the filial deprivation experience may have predictive value with regard to eventual return of children to their own homes. It appears reasonable to hypothesize that part of the readjustment problem of children who go home may reflect not only separation trauma but also the reception from their parents. In some instances the family may, in a sense, have closed in behind the separated child, and there may be neither psychological nor physical space for him when he returns to his former home.

The present chapter has a broad-based approach to the subject of filial deprivation. Background studies from psychological and social work literature will be reviewed before description of the research approach of this study. Data reported in the chapter relate to feelings and feeling referents of mothers and fathers in the study sample, and factor analysis is used to integrate these findings. A final section presents results on a cluster analysis of data, an innovative technique to explore feeling patterns and relate them to other characteristics of parent groups.

LITERATURE RELATED TO
PARENTAL FEELINGS

The literature on maternal deprivation is singularly barren with regard to feelings, reactions, and roles of natural parents when children enter care. This review of the rather fragmentary literature serves as background for the concept of deprivation as utilized in the family study.

Bowlby in *Maternal Care and Mental Health* was concerned with the effect of severe privation and deprivation on the emotional and personality growth of the child. He did, however, refer to the "vicious circle" resulting from unsympathetic handling by the mother when the returned child displays regressive, anxious behavior and noted how "bad behavior" brings rebuffs which, in turn, result in further "bad behavior." [3] The deprivation literature does not examine experiences of mothers who cope with the problems of having a separated child. Some references to parent-child interaction, however, have relevance for understanding situations of foster care placement. Prugh and Harlow, in discussing "masked deprivation," refer to what they term "distorted relatedness" and "insufficient relatedness" on the part of parent to child. As one instance of the latter, they report that "situational factors involving current reality problems may produce psychological disorders in the parent which may affect detrimentally the developmental processes of the infant." [4]

Some of the experimental studies of animal behavior contain observations which, although not immediately generalizable to humans, raise some relevant questions about separation experiences. Blauvelt, for example, in her study "Neonate-Mother Relationship in Goat and Man," describes how the mother establishes a "territory," or safe area, near herself for her newborn kid. She reports that when separation of mother and newborn is achieved experimentally by introducing unexpected distracting or frightening stimuli, "if the mother and her newborn are not free to

3. John Bowlby, *Maternal Care and Mental Health* (Geneva, World Health Organization, 1952), p. 26.
4. Dane G. Prugh and R. G. Harlow, "Masked Deprivation in Infants and Young Children," in *Deprivation of Maternal Care* (Geneva, World Health Organization, 1962), p. 19.

reestablish the normal pattern in the ways that are natural to them, it is possible that the mother animal will be unable to give the young the care essential for its survival at a later period." [5] In describing readjustment problems of kittens after an experimental period of isolation from the mother, Rosenblatt, Schneirla, and Turkewitz report on the changing patterns of maternal-young relations in the litter period, and state that "the litter situation confronting isolates returned from the brooder at different times differed radically from that prevalent at the earlier time of removal, especially as concerned the general behavior of the female [mother] and her responses to the kittens." The disturbed behavior in formerly isolated kittens was not a result of their experience in the brooder but of their inability, upon return to the litter, to make an appropriate adjustment to the different pattern of the mother cat.[6]

Harlow, in reporting on "The Maternal Affectional System of Rhesus Monkeys," identified the point on the hypothetical graph of mother and infant contact needs when intensity is reversed, and the infant's needs exceed the mother's. In an interpretation both alliterative and lyrical he states, "As attachment abates, ambivalence arises and anticipates alienation," and he goes on to say:

> From here on mother does not care
> For baby fingers in her hair;

5. Helen Blauvelt, "Neonate-Mother Relationship in Goat and Man," in *Group Processes,* ed. Bertram Schaffner (New York, Josiah Macy, Jr. Foundation, 1956), pp. 113–16.
6. Jay S. Rosenblatt, T. C. Schneirla, and G. Turkewitz, "Early Socialization in the Domestic Cat as Based on Feeding and Other Relationships between Female and Young," in *Determinants of Infant Behavior,* ed. Brian Foss (London, Methuen, 1961), p. 72.

A touch that once went to her heart
Now merely makes the hair depart.[7]

The social work literature, like the separation material, stresses the child in placement, with concern being focused primarily on practical service problems and plans for care. Appropriate placements, the use of foster family or institutional care, and agency practices are widely debated. There has been a historical separation of "family" from "child welfare" agencies, leaving little room for the concept of "child and family" (whether living apart or together), and only in recent years has there been a new emphasis on the importance of working with natural mothers as a precursor to eventual family reunion.

Although a review of the literature has not indicated any systematic study of parental reactions to separation from their children, several references have been made to feelings of parents when children are placed in care. Aptekar, for example, in discussing casework with the child's own family, notes "Every parent . . . reacts in his own individual way—with his own personality and in the context of his own living problems—to . . . the placement experience. All of his important problems and all of his chief character traits will come out in relation to the placement. . . ." [8] In a discussion of casework techniques, Britton states "In all cases where parents have failed to keep their children there is a tremendous sense of guilt which can be completely par-

7. Harry F. Harlow, M. K. Harlow, and E. W. Hansen, "The Maternal Affectional System of Rhesus Monkeys," in *Maternal Behavior in Mammals,* ed. Harriet L. Rheingold (New York, John Wiley, 1963), p. 279.
8. Herbert H. Aptekar, *Casework with the Child's Own Family in Child Placing Agencies* (New York, Child Welfare League of America, 1953), p. 47.

alyzing . . . The result of this feeling is apathy and depression or the projection of their feelings onto some external factor or person whom they seek to blame for what has happened. The sense of guilt and resulting hopelessness can be so great that they repudiate the relationship altogether and feel no sense of responsibility." [9] The feeling of guilt is also noted by Clarice Freud, who states "In placement a parent is separating from a part of himself, a part of himself which he may partly love and partly hate. . . . His guilt, which is a feeling usually most evident, is based on what he is doing to his child and is also in terms of social disapproval. Perhaps most profound is his sense of inadequacy." [10] Glickman sees the "separation trauma" as meaning to the parent failure in responsibility, first as a parent and then as an individual.[11] In discussing request for placement, Hutchinson points out that such a request contradicts both the code of parental behavior and the code of society.[12] According to Smith, Ricketts, and Smith,[13] parents who are questioned in a child guidance clinic about their experiences on and after separation expressed some relief from tension, but also feelings of intense loneliness,

9. Clare Britton, "Casework Techniques in Child Care Services," *Social Casework,* 36, No. 1 (January 1955), p. 12.

10. Clarice Freud, "Meaning of Separation to Parents and Children as Seen in Child Placement," *Public Welfare,* 13, No. 1 (January 1955), p. 15.

11. Esther Glickman, "Treatment of the Child and His Family After Placement," *Social Service Review,* 28, No. 3 (September 1954), pp. 279–89.

12. Dorothy Hutchinson, "The Request for Placement has Meaning," *Social Casework,* 25, No. 4 (June 1944), pp. 128–32.

13. Emily A. Smith, B. M. Ricketts, and S. H. Smith, "The Recommendation for Child Placement by a Psychiatric Clinic," *American Journal of Orthopsychiatry,* 32, No. 1 (January 1962), pp. 42–49.

emptiness and guilt. One descriptive phrase used was that the child's placement felt "like a death." Young, in discussing separation, states that parents who fail become objects of scorn in the community, since parenthood is a responsibility of our culture, and placement tends to be an admission that individuals have failed as parents.[14]

One interesting reaction is noted by Mandelbaum, who discusses the significance of placement to parents whose children are in residential treatment and reports feelings of isolation, loneliness, and inadequacy expressed by these parents when separation takes place. He states that some parents anticipate punishment, expressing the fear that children will grow "big and powerful" in placement and will destroy parents when they return home as retaliation for their having allowed placement to occur.[15]

These observations from the social work literature are interesting as points of reference; but they are limited by lack of systematic study and by the varying nature of the populations upon which they are based. The present research provided an opportunity for systematic access to a wide range of placing parents as well as to many families whose children entered care precipitously with little or no planning and sometimes even without their knowledge. The design is comprehensive enough both vertically, in the initial cohort, and horizontally, in its longitudinal phases, to secure data hopefully broad enough to derive generalizations for the overall field.

14. Leontine R. Young, *Separation: Its Meaning to the Child, the Parents, and the Community* (New York State Conference of Social Work Proceedings 1943–1945, Annual Volume 1945), pp. 52–61.
15. Arthur Mandelbaum, "Parent-Child Separation: Its Significance to Parents," *Social Work*, 7, No. 4 (October 1962), pp. 26–34.

FEELINGS CHOSEN FOR STUDY

The particular feelings chosen for study were selected after extensive exploratory work and pretesting with parents not in the sample but in comparable circumstances who had experienced separation. These exploratory interviews with parents, shortly after the initial placement experience, began with a review of the problems which brought the child into care; then the interviewer said, "We would like to understand more about how people feel when their children go into placement away from home. How about you, how did you feel the day your child was placed?" The request for an immediate reaction on the day of placement was introduced to focus the respondent in time and secure data on the impact of separation. In the study proper this provided baseline information for later discussion of changes in feelings.

After a general statement of feelings at the time of placement, respondents were then asked to describe in just one word their strongest feeling on that particular day. From these spontaneous statements made in the exploratory field interviews, a check list was developed for the final schedule.

The feelings studied in the actual field interviews with the study sample are:

sad	thankful	paralyzed
angry	worried	ashamed
bitter	nervous	empty
relieved	guilty	numb

A respondent could report from 0 to all 12 feelings as having been experienced on the day the child was placed. Feeling referents, or the main objects of each feeling, were also investigated. A mother, for example, would be asked, "Were you worried on the day your child was placed?" If she said "Yes," the interviewer would proceed to ask, "About what?" Similarly, she was asked, "Did you feel guilty?" If the answer was "Yes," she was asked, "About what?" Spontaneous responses to the referent question were recorded by the social work interviewer in the client's own words. Analysis of the response patterns led to their being categorized by judges along 7 main dimensions. These are:

self   agency
self-child or separation   other interpersonal
child   generalized other or
child-agency or agency-care   society

Each of the 12 feelings could have a referent in any one of these 7 categories. An example of how answers to "What were you worried about?" might refer to each of the categories, respectively, can be seen from the hypothetical responses:

"What will happen to me" (self)
"Being away from my child" (separation)
"If my child is happy" (child)
"If they will take care of him" (agency-care)
"What those workers are like" (agency)
"If my husband will come back" (interpersonal)
"About everything" (generalized other)

FREQUENCIES OF FEELING RESPONSES. Sadness is the major feeling reported in parental responses, as shown in Table IV.1. Also high in frequency among the feelings ex-

TABLE IV.1

Parental Feelings Reported as
Experienced on Day of Placement

Feeling	Percent of mothers (N = 297)	Percent of fathers (N = 137)
sad	87	90
worried	74	68
nervous	68	56
empty	60	42
angry	50	45
bitter	43	43
thankful	42	57
relieved	40	42
guilty	39	30
ashamed	36	39
numb	19	14
paralyzed	16	11

pressed are worry and nervousness. From 40 to 60 percent of both mothers and fathers reported feelings of emptiness, anger, bitterness, thankfulness, and relief. Relatively few parents reported numbness or the feeling of being paralyzed.

Although differences can be seen in the relative extent to which mothers (N = 297) and fathers (N = 137) report various feelings, male-female contrasts are not made between these groups because of the differences in sample size.[16] A systematic bias may be introduced because of the

16. For those 88 families where both mothers and fathers of the same child were interviewed, a separate comparative analysis of responses is made in Chapter 6, "Parental Pairs."

lack of accessibility to the most pathological fathers and the number of cases where the identities of fathers or their whereabouts were unknown.

CORRELATES OF FEELINGS. In the initial field interviews in the family study, data were collected on over a thousand variables, and one task was to identify which of these many characteristics of the sample were significantly related to feelings at placement. Among the variables whose possible associations with the feeling data were studied were jurisdiction of case, ethnic group of parent, reason for placement, and parental perception of necessity of placement. The feeling data refer primarily to the 297 interviewed mothers, since this group is most broadly representative of the total study sample.

Jurisdiction of case is a variable that is defined at the point of entry, although it may shift at a later time. Approximately 19 percent of all mothers had children who entered the study under the supervision of the Family Court, and the remaining 81 percent had children who entered through the Bureau of Child Welfare of the Department of Social Services. When these groupings were compared, mothers whose children entered through the Family Court were significantly [17] more angry and more nervous than the others, whereas mothers who were Bureau of Child Welfare clients were significantly more relieved and more thankful about the placement. It is of interest that there was no significant difference with regard to guilt, although the most severe abuse and neglect situations occurred among the Court children. A comparison was made between feeling

17. To determine "significant" differences the chi-square test was used with $P \leq .05$.

responses of mothers whose children had been placed directly from the hospital and responses of those who were placed from homes. The respondents in the former instance were primarily unwed mothers who had left their babies. Significantly fewer such mothers reported nervousness and bitterness than mothers whose children had been in their own care or in the care of others in the community. Guilt was not significantly more common for mothers leaving newborn infants.

Although ethnic group of respondent and reason for placement tend to be interrelated, feelings were analyzed separately in relation to each of these two variables. It will be recalled that, of the 297 mothers, 27 percent were white, 42 percent black, and 31 percent Puerto Rican. It is of interest that when feelings were compared by ethnic group, significant differences were found for 8 of the 12 feeling dimensions. The feelings for which there were no significant differences relevant to ethnic group were sadness, emptiness, anger, and guilt. Significant differences, however, were found for thankfulness, which was more characteristic of the white and Puerto Rican groups and less characteristic of the black group; and worry, less common for the white group and more common for the black and Puerto Rican groups. The feeling of paralysis, although limited, tended to be expressed significantly more frequently by Puerto Rican mothers. Bitterness was less typical of the black group and significantly more typical of the Puerto Rican group. Shame and nervousness were expressed by significantly fewer whites and more blacks. Relief, on the other hand, was expressed by significantly more whites and fewer blacks and Puerto Ricans.

Within ethnic groups two questions were examined. The

stereotype that white Jewish mothers might feel more guilty on placement of their children than other white mothers was examined and found not to be valid. The difference between 19 white Jewish mothers and 69 other white mothers with regard to guilt was not significant. On the other hand, significant differences emerged between 30 black Catholic and 93 black Protestant mothers. The percent of black Catholic mothers who expressed anger was found to be significantly higher than the percent of black Protestant mothers who expressed anger. This is of interest in relation to data presented in Chapter 2, which showed households of black Catholic children to be in better socioeconomic circumstances than those of black Protestant children.

The impoverished conditions of the overall study sample, of whom 45 percent were supported primarily by public assistance, have been described in Chapter 2. When the associations between socioeconomic level and feeling data were examined, identification was made of four feeling dimensions where significant differences were observed. A significantly greater percent of mothers with relatively higher socioeconomic circumstances were thankful and relieved upon placement. In contrast, a greater proportion of mothers with relatively low socioeconomic circumstances were nervous and worried on the day their child was placed.

In the field interview, mothers were asked to react, on a five-point scale, to the question "How necessary was it that your child enter placement?" The range of responses secured was as follows: "absolutely," 37 percent; "very," 21 percent; "somewhat," 18 percent; "not at all," 24 percent. When feelings were related to maternal perceptions of necessity of placement several significant associations emerged.

The more "necessary" mothers viewed placement, the more commonly they said they had been thankful and relieved on the day the child entered care, but relatively fewer expressed feelings of emptiness or worry. On the other hand, mothers who said placement was not at all necessary tended more characteristically to be angry, ashamed, and bitter.

In several aspects of the study, the reason for placement was a critical variable.[18] Feelings, as well, were significantly related to reason for placement in a whole series of instances. Thankfulness, for example, was significantly more common, and guilt and anger significantly less common, when children were placed because of the physical illness of the mother. When placement was because of child behavior problems, however, both guilt and relief were significantly more characteristic and anger and bitterness less characteristic. It is ironic, but understandable, that anger was expressed by significantly more mothers when children entered care because of severe neglect and abuse by parents or for reasons of family dysfunction, including conflict, alcoholism, drugs, and incompetence, than for other reasons. Finally, the feeling of shame was significantly more characteristic of those families whose children were placed because of family dysfunction.

REFERENTS OF EXPRESSED FEELINGS

The data from the respondents on referents of feelings indicate that certain feelings were strongly organized in specific directions to individuals or institutions in the person's life

18. See Chapter 3 for a full discussion of rationale for identification of reasons.

TABLE IV.2

Percent Distribution of Referents for Feelings Experienced by Mothers (N = 297)

Feeling	Total	Self	Self-child	Child	Inter-personal	Agency care	Generalized other	Agency	Not known
sad	100	9	69	8	—	6	5	—	3
angry	100	13	—	3	53	—	5	25	1
relieved	100	11	3	12	3	66	1	2	2
nervous	100	16	31	14	1	13	16	5	4
ashamed	100	59	13	4	6	2	13	2	1
numb	100	25	29	5	3	2	27	2	7
empty	100	13	77	2	2	1	2	—	3
bitter	100	17	—	1	55	—	9	16	2
thankful	100	5	3	9	1	61	—	20	1
worried	100	6	28	30	2	28	2	3	1
guilty	100	84	5	2	1	2	2	—	4
paralyzed	100	42	24	6	6	—	14	2	6

TABLE IV.3

Percent Distribution of Referents for Feelings
Experienced by Fathers (N = 137)

Referent

Feeling	Total	Self	Self-child	Child	Inter-personal	Agency care	Generalized other	Agency	Not known
sad	100	3	62	19	2	6	6	—	2
angry	100	13	—	3	61	—	3	20	—
relieved	100	5	3	14	3	68	—	—	7
nervous	100	22	15	24	—	19	18	2	—
ashamed	100	53	11	4	13	2	13	—	4
numb	100	10	27	—	—	10	48	—	5
empty	100	12	80	—	2	2	2	—	2
bitter	100	15	2	—	56	—	15	12	—
thankful	100	2	1	4	5	68	—	19	1
worried	100	2	17	41	6	25	6	2	1
guilty	100	94	2	—	2	—	2	—	—
paralyzed	100	27	19	7	7	—	27	—	13

experience, whereas others were diffused. This can be seen in the percentage distributions of feeling referents for mothers and fathers in Tables IV.2 and IV.3. The most focused of the feelings appeared to be the feeling of guilt, its primary referent being self for 84 percent of mothers and 94 percent of fathers. The feeling of sadness was referred to the separation experience by 69 percent of mothers and 62 percent of fathers. The other substantial referent of sadness was the child, noted by 19 percent of fathers and 8 percent of mothers.

The feeling of anger was primarily interpersonal, with 53 percent of angry mothers and 61 percent of angry fathers expressing their anger against another person in their life situation, frequently the absent partner or another relative. Bitterness was also primarily interpersonal, and was so reported by 55 percent of mothers and 56 percent of fathers. Feelings of relief and thankfulness were expressed in relation to agency care of the child by over 60 percent of mothers and fathers. Shame was referred to self by 59 percent of mothers and 53 percent of fathers. Emptiness was referred to the separation by 77 percent of mothers and 80 percent of fathers.

Nervousness was diffuse, and associated by mothers and fathers with several referents, including the separation, themselves, the child, agency care, and "just everything." Worry was a feeling which also had a variety of referents, being expressed in terms of the child, the agency care, and the separation. The distribution of referents for worry was comparable to the distribution on the dimension of nervousness, except that there were fewer self-referents.

These distributions indicate that referents may be either highly concentrated or diffused, depending on the feeling dimension. Those feelings with high specificity of referent were sadness, anger, relief, shame, emptiness, bitterness, thankfulness, and guilt. Those feelings which were diffused were nervousness, numbness, worry, and paralysis. In summary, anger and bitterness were primarily interpersonal; guilt had the most highly concentrated self-referent, more so than shame; thankfulness and relief were agency-focused; and worry and nervousness tended to be diffused, indicating generalized anxiety.

When referents are viewed without regard to particular feelings, the data show that 28 percent of all feelings expressed by both parents referred to the separation experience, 20 percent to self, and 17 percent to agency care. The child himself and "other interpersonal" each comprised 11 percent of all referents. Seven percent of feelings referred to "generalized other," and 6 percent to the agency itself. This distribution gives some insight regarding the channels into which feelings flow and the direction of the emotional reactions at the time of separation.

FACTOR ANALYSIS OF
FEELING-REFERENTS

Feelings and referents having been analyzed separately, the next step was to examine their relationships and identify any systematic patterns of organization. One question was whether specific feelings and referents were highly associated with each other and appeared together in a fairly consistent pattern. If they did, it would be relevant to ask if the groups of associated feeling-referents could be characterized as factors, and if their identification would contribute to the understanding of parental reactions when children entered care.

For this purpose the intercorrelations of the feeling-referents were factor-analyzed.[19] This is a statistical procedure in which the relationships among a set of variables are studied in order to identify a smaller number of "factors" which account for the interrelationships among the variables. The identification of these factors is an aid in interpreting interrelationships in the data. Since there are 12 feelings, each with a choice of 7 referents, there is a large number of possible feeling-referent combinations. Referents, however, tend to be more highly concentrated for certain feelings than for others, so it was decided that no feeling-referent pair which drew fewer than ten responses from either mothers or fathers would be included in the factor analysis. This reduced the total number of variables in the correlation matrix to approximately 40.

Separate correlation matrices were prepared for mothers and for fathers. The patterns of intercorrelation for male as against female parents were different enough to warrant application of independent factor analyses to each group. Based on these factor analyses, six factors were identified for mothers, and three factors were identified for fathers.

For mothers, the following six factors were indicated: (I) interpersonal hostility; (II) separation anxiety with sadness; (III) self-denigration; (IV) agency hostility; (V) concerned

19. The procedure applied was based on the *Data-Text System, A Computer Language for Social Science Research* (developed at Harvard University, Department of Social Relations, 1967). It consisted of a principal components analysis followed by rotation according to the Varimax criterion.

gratitude; and (VI) self-involvement. For the fathers, the following three factors were identified: (I) separation anxiety with numbness; (II) personal shame with relief about care; and (III) personal guilt with interpersonal hostility. The major variables associated with each factor are shown in Table IV. 4.

Examination of the identifiable factors noted for mothers suggests that there is strong evidence of a pattern of self-concern and self-involvement, as well as of hostility both to agency and to persons in their life situations. Father factors tend to refer to feelings of personal shame and personal guilt; they also tend to be less self-referred and more child and child-care oriented. This interpretation may reflect the fact that the mother is more personally involved in the placement situation and sees it more in relation to herself and her child-caring role. The fathers interviewed were less personally involved as child-caring individuals and saw placement as a reflection of their inadequate social performance and their social failure.

CLUSTER ANALYSIS OF
FEELING DATA

The factor analysis technique, although it identifies higher order "factors" among feeling-referent combinations, does not provide an answer to a further critical question—how mothers and fathers may be grouped in terms of the individual constellations of each parent's own feeling patterns. The data show that parents have conflicting feelings, and their responses and reactions are complex. The research

TABLE IV.4

Results of Factor Analysis of Placement-Day Feelings
and Referents Reported by Mothers and Fathers

MOTHER FACTORS

Factor	Variable	Loading[a]
I. Interpersonal hostility	Empty: self-child	.35
	Angry: interpersonal	.78
	Bitter: interpersonal	.82
II. Separation anxiety with sadness	Sad: self-child	.54
	Worried: self-child	.64
	Nervous: self-child	.55
	Paralyzed: self-child	.31
	Numb: self-child	.36
III. Self-denigration	Sad: self	(−) .43
	Angry: self	(−) .55
	Ashamed: self	(−) .65
	Bitter: self	(−) .42
	Guilt: self	(−) .66
IV. Agency hostility	Not sad: Agency care	(−) .35
	Not relieved: agency care	(−) .32
	Not thankful: agency care	(−) .43
	Angry: agency	.65
	Nervous: agency	.38
	Bitter: agency	.62
V. Concerned gratitude	Worried: child	.60
	Not worried: agency care	(−) .62
	Thankful: agency	.36

question, posed in statistical terms for computer analysis, was whether these individual reaction patterns could be identified and grouped into a typology of parental feeling syndromes. Furthermore, if such syndromes could be identified, were they related to other variables and to characteristics of the parent population? Thus, the task was to identify individual clusters of feelings which groups of parents held in common. The hypothesis was that although there was no unique or single continuum of feelings experienced

TABLE IV.4 (*continued*)

MOTHER FACTORS

Factor	*Variable*	*Loading*[a]
VI. Self-involvement	Numb: self	.33
	Empty: self	.53
	Worried: self	.35
	Not sad: child	(−) .38
	Thankful: child	.34
	Bitter: generalized other	.34

FATHER FACTORS

I. Separation anxiety with numbness	Nervous: self-child	.59
	Worried: self-child	.97
	Numb: generalized other	.97
II. Personal shame with relief about care	Ashamed: self	.86
	Relieved: agency care	.62
	Nervous: agency care	.82
	Thankful: agency care	.30
III. Personal guilt with interpersonal hostility	Guilty: self	.66
	Sad: child	.56
	Angry: interpersonal	.41
	Bitter: interpersonal	.57

[a] Factor loadings express the estimated correlation between the individual variables and the underlying factor. They range between −1.00 and +1.00. For each factor, variables with a loading of at least ±.30 are noted.

by any parent, parents would fall in distinct groupings based on combinations of feelings.

The technique of cluster analysis was selected for application to the data. Cluster analysis represents a procedure specifically designed to find the optimal way of organizing a set of objects into groups based on internal similarities, with no prior hypothesis of anticipated relationships. Each object, i.e., case, is represented by a set of observations, i.e., feeling responses. The task of the computer program is to partition the sets of cases according to the similarity of responses among them.[20]

The application in the present study of this program for cluster analysis to psychosocial data represents an innovative approach. In the past the technique has been applied primarily to the biological and physical sciences, e.g., to group symptoms related to disease patterns,[21] to gain new ways of looking at various types of cardiac malfunction,[22] or to classify varieties of plant life.[23]

The unique utility of the cluster analysis technique for the feeling data of the family study is that it represents an internal operation which develops clusters in terms of the most useful arrangement of all observations, rather than analyzing them against an independent variable which is external to the data. Thus it is not hypothesis testing. It differs from the procedure of correlation analysis, where a single variable may be related to one or more other variables. There is no assumption here that associations exist on a continuum of "more or less" relatedness. There is correspondence with the factor analysis technique, but the differ-

20. For background literature on cluster analysis see A. W. F. Edwards and L. L. Cavalli-Sforza, "A Method for Cluster Analysis," *Biometrics,* 21, 1965; and J. Rubin, "Application of Cluster Analysis to Medical Data" (Mathematics and Applications Department, International Business Machines Corporation, April 1964).

21. D. N. Baron and Patricia M. Fraser, "The Digital Computer in the Classification of Diseases," *The Lancet,* November 1965, pp. 1066–69.

22. Arthur Lemlitch, Herman Ziffer, Herman P. Friedman, Jerrold Rubin, and Lester Talkington, "Acute Myocardial Infarction: New Mathematical Approaches" (American Medical Association, San Francisco, June 21–25, 1964).

23. David J. Rogers and Taffee T. Tanimoto, "A Computer Program for Classifying Plants," *Science,* October 1960, pp. 1115–18.

ence is that it is possible to relate patterns or clusters of individuals with correspondence to each other, rather than merely identifying patterns or factors of feelings which hold together. As already noted, the factor analysis of the feeling data shows what feelings go together, but not by individual respondents. The cluster analysis, on the other hand, shows which individuals go together in terms of similarity of their patterned responses.[24]

RESULTS OF THE CLUSTER ANALYSIS OF MOTHER'S FEELINGS ON DAY OF PLACEMENT. The initial cluster analysis procedure resulted in the identification of seven groups of mothers partitioned on the basis of common patterns of feeling responses. The number of mothers in six of the groups ranged from three to fifty, but the seventh group included 172 cases. Eight feelings were predominant in that large group, namely sadness, emptiness, anger, bitterness, worry, nervousness, shame, and guilt. A further clustering procedure was done for that group of 172 cases which resulted in the identification of seven subclusters which, although they shared the larger common core of anxiety-hostility-guilt feelings, nonetheless had separate subsidiary feeling patterns. These two clustering procedures, therefore, isolated a total of thirteen groups of mothers with distinguishable feeling patterns. In three of those thirteen groups

---

24. The computer program utilized for the cluster analysis procedures undertaken by the present study was the "Optimal Taxonomy Program for the 7090 IBM 0026" (Share General Program Library, International Business Machines Corporation). The procedure was applied only to the data on feelings and not to referents of feelings. The latter were excluded because of the large number of possible feeling-referent combinations.

the number of cases was so small that analysis of them was handicapped. In two other groups the "stability" (the statistical internal integrity) [25] was so low that it was not possible to identify constellations of feelings unique to them. The eight remaining cluster groups, which include a total of 237 mothers, are presented in Chart 1. The chart presents the predominant feelings expressed by mothers in each of those eight groups on the day their children entered placement, as well as the feelings that were significantly absent in each group.

The identification of feeling clusters was useful not only in understanding parental reactions, but in providing a single descriptive measure to relate to other important study variables. In order to determine whether there were other characteristics common to mothers in each cluster, frequency distributions of nine critical descriptive variables were obtained for each group. The descriptive variables are: predominant ethnic group; socioeconomic level; primary reason for placement; mother's judgment of the necessity for the placement; jurisdiction of the case; age of the child at the time of the placement; continuance of the child in placement for more or less than a full year; mother's

25. The cluster analysis program selects clusters of cases which are most similar to each other on selected variables. The degree of similarity, however, can range from marginal to excellent. Although a case may be relatively most similar to cases in its own cluster, it can also range from being quite similar to totally dissimilar to cases in another cluster. The extent to which cases in a particular cluster are similar to their own group or "pulled by" similarity to cases in other groups is indicated by a measure called the stability coefficient of the specific cluster. As noted above, the stability of two of the thirteen isolated cluster groups was very poor. Those two groups were therefore eliminated from this analysis.

score on an index of alienation; and predominant attitude of mother to the placement agencies.[26]

This cross-tabulation of cluster groups and descriptive variables was a truly exploratory effort, relating and comparing different sets of measurements. Because of the small size of the groups and the multiplicity and scatter of the variables, it was not anticipated that hard, sharply defined lines could be drawn. Determination of feeling clusters, for example, is complicated by the fact that the same feelings appear in several cluster groups, although the constellations of feelings may be differently patterned. Such a dilemma is not unlike that faced in medical diagnosis, which may serve as a relevant analogy. A range of symptoms such as fever, breathing difficulties, and weakness appear in a multiplicity of diseases, e.g., the common cold, influenza, pneumonia. This does not mean that the disease pattern is the same for each, even though there is duplication of some symptoms. The cluster analysis technique accepts the nature of parental emotional life, which is that commonalities as well as contradictions of feelings are expressed, but hypothesizes that nonetheless patterns of feelings may be distinctly identified. The designation of eight clusters which when statistically tested were significantly different from the feeling distribution for the sample as a whole supports this hypothesis.

In the present analysis the clusters were related to nine descriptive variables, each variable being categorized by a differing number of categories. With regard to discharge, for example, there are two categories—in or out of placement after one year; with regard to ethnic group, there are three,

26. The derivations of the last two variables shown in the chart (mother's score on an index of alienation, and predominant attitude of mother to the placement agencies) are discussed in detail in Chapter 5.

CHART 1

Mother Cluster Groups: Feelings and Descriptive Variables

Cluster group	Feelings on day of placement [a]		Feelings significantly absent [c]	Predominant ethnic group	Socio-economic level	Primary reasons for placement
	Predominant feelings [c]					
A (N = 26)	Relieved Thankful		Angry Bitter Ashamed Nervous Worried	White [c]	High [c]	Unwillingness or inability to assume care [c] Child behavior
B (N = 50)	Thankful Worried		Angry Bitter Ashamed Guilty Nervous Paralyzed Empty	Puerto Rican [c]	—	Child behavior Physical illness
C (N = 21)	Sad Empty	Empty Angry Bitter Nervous Numb Paralyzed	Relieved	Puerto Rican [c]	—	Unwillingness or inability to continue care Family dysfunction
D (N = 18)	Angry Bitter	Empty Worried Ashamed Guilty Relieved Thankful Numb Paralyzed	—	White and Puerto Rican [c]	—	Mental illness Child behavior
E (N = 51)	Nervous	Empty Angry Bitter Worried Ashamed Guilty	Thankful	Black [c]	Middle [d]	Abandonment or desertion [c] Family dysfunction
F (N = 19)	Worried	Empty Worried Ashamed	Angry Bitter Relieved	Black [c]	Low	Unwillingness or inability to assume care Family dysfunction
G (N = 30)	Ashamed	Angry Nervous Worried	Ashamed Guilty Thankful Numb	—	—	Neglect and abuse [c]
H (N = 22)	Guilty	Empty Nervous Worried Relieved Thankful	Ashamed Guilty	—	—	Physical illness [c] Unwillingness or inability to continue care [c]

[a] Significant differences in feelings for Groups A and B were determined by comparing them with the total sample. Significant differences for the remaining groups were determined by comparing them with the total cases in Groups C through H.

[b] Descriptive variables when footnoted are statistically significant as noted below. Where they are not footnoted the proportion of cases in the cate-

Mothers' opinion of necessity of placement	Juris-diction of case	Age of child at placement	Child in placement at least one year	Alien-ation score	Pre-dominant agency attitude
Absolutely [e]	BCW	—	Yes [d]	Low [e]	—
Absolutely [e]	—	6 or more [e]	—	—	Surrogate
Somewhat [e]	—	Under 2	Yes	—	Usurper
Somewhat	—	6 or more [d]	No	Middle	—
Not at all [e]	—	2 to under 6	—	High [e]	—
Somewhat Not at all	—	2 to under 6	No	Middle	—
Not at all [e]	Court [e]	Under 6 [e]	No	High	Usurper
Absolutely Very	BCW	—	—	—	—

gory in the cluster is at least one third greater than the proportion of cases in the category in the total sample.

[e] Significant difference from total sample at $P \leqslant .05$ using Chi square with Yates continuity correction.

[d] Significant difference from total sample at $.05 < P \leqslant .10$ using Chi square with Yates continuity correction.

black, white or Puerto Rican; for reason for placement, there are nine possibilities. With the small size of each cluster, from 18 to 50 cases, it is apparent that any variable with a large number of categories, such as reason for placement, may be broken into cells with numbers in each too small for statistical testing.

Among the categories and findings set forth in Chart 1, therefore, certain variations have been noted. The diagram shows clusters and predominant categories observed for nine critical variables. Differences are significant at either the $P \leq .05$ or the $.05 < P \leq .10$ levels, as indicated. Categories that were observed to be suggestive of relationships, but were not statistically significant when tested are also noted. The criterion for including such instances was that the proportion of cases in the category for the cluster group had to be at least one-third greater than the proportion for the sample as a whole in that category.

On the left of the diagram, cluster groups with feelings significantly present and absent ($P \leq .05$) are identified. Relatively more mothers in Cluster A, for example, felt relieved and thankful the day their child was placed than mothers in any other group. Cluster B was also generally thankful, but instead of being relieved they were worried. Clusters C through H had as a frame of reference the anxiety-hostility-guilt component, but they were differentiated from each other on combinations of other feelings. For Cluster G, for example, it was anger, nervousness, and worry; for Cluster C it was anger and nervousness with emptiness, numbness, bitterness, and paralysis; for Cluster F it was shame, worry, and emptiness.

Each of the eight cluster groups is described in detail

below, supplementing the chart definitions. Emphasis in the descriptions is given to the predominant characteristics of each group, including suggestive differences and those which were statistically significant. The descriptions are suggestive for further research.

DESCRIPTION OF MOTHER CLUSTERS. *Cluster A:* The predominant feelings of the mothers in Cluster A were relief and thankfulness. Significantly absent were feelings of anger, bitterness, shame, nervousness, and worry. There were significantly more white mothers and mothers of relatively high socioeconomic status (for this sample) in this group. Placement occurred primarily because the mother was unwilling to assume care of the child, who in most such cases was born out of wedlock. There was also a large proportion of cases where the child was placed because of his or her own behavior. The Bureau of Child Welfare rather than the Court tended to have jurisdiction over these cases at the time of entry. One year after placement a significant number of these children were still in care. The mothers in this cluster generally saw placement as having been absolutely necessary, and they scored low on the scale designed to measure degree of alienation.

Cluster B: The mothers in this cluster felt thankful, but also worried, the day their child was placed. Significantly absent were feelings of anger, bitterness, shame, guilt, emptiness, nervousness, and paralysis. This cluster was significantly Puerto Rican in ethnic composition. No single socioeconomic level predominated, similar proportions of mothers in this group being of high, middle, and low status. Physical illness of the child-caring person and child behavior tended to be the primary reasons for placement. The placed child was older, usually six years or more. The mothers in this cluster saw placement as absolutely necessary and tended to view placement agencies as surrogate parents.

Cluster C: Anger, bitterness, numbness, and paralysis were the predominant feelings of the mothers in Cluster C, along with emptiness and nervousness. Data on feeling referents, not included in the diagram, show the anger of this group to be mainly interpersonal, directed against relatives or friends. Absent was any significant level of relief at placement. The mothers in this cluster were predominantly Puerto Rican. Their children tended to enter foster care because the child-caring person was unwilling or unable to continue care or because of family dysfunction. At the time of placement the children were generally under two years of age. They tended to remain in placement at least a year. In the mothers' opinion the placement was usually considered to be only somewhat necessary, and placement agencies tended to be seen as usurpers of child care.

Although Clusters B and C are both made up predominantly of Puerto Rican mothers, they differ considerably in the feelings they had at the time of placement, the reasons their children were originally placed, their judgment of the necessity of placement, the ages of their children at placement, and their attitudes toward foster care agencies.

Cluster D: The mothers in this cluster shared a very large number of feelings on the day their child entered placement. Along with emptiness and worry were feelings of relief, thankfulness, shame, guilt, numbness, and paralysis. Puerto Rican and white mothers made up most of this cluster, with relatively few black mothers included. Mental illness of the child-caring person or behavior problems of the child were the primary reasons for placement. The children tended to be older, six years or more, and to stay in placement less than a full year. These mothers tended to see placement as having been only somewhat necessary. As a group these mothers tended to score in the middle range of the alienation scale.

Cluster E: Anger and bitterness, commingled with feelings of emptiness, worry, shame, and guilt, were characteristic of this cluster. Significantly absent were feelings of thankfulness. The anger felt by this group was mainly interpersonal, directed against relatives. Black mothers of middle socioeconomic level were significantly predominant in this cluster. Abandonment or desertion and family dysfunction were the primary reasons for placement. The children tended to be young, between two and six years of age; the mothers in this cluster saw placement as not at all necessary; and they scored high on the alienation scale.

Cluster F: Shame, emptiness, and worry predominated as feelings for this cluster. Anger, bitterness, and relief were significantly absent. Black mothers of low socioeconomic status made up the greater part of the membership of this cluster. Family dysfunction and unwillingness or inability to assume care (out-of-wedlock births) tended to be the main reasons for placement. The children were young, generally between two and six years of age, and tended to remain in care less than a year. The mothers in this cluster generally saw placement as only somewhat or not at all necessary. As a group they tended to score in the middle range of the scale measuring alienation.

Although Clusters E and F are both made up predominantly of black mothers, they differ markedly in many respects. Both groups felt emptiness, worry, and shame. However, Cluster E felt anger and bitterness while those feelings were significantly absent from Cluster F. The mothers of Cluster E are predominantly of middle socioeconomic status, whereas Cluster F mothers are predominantly of low socioeconomic level. One of the primary reasons for placement in both groups was family dysfunction. For Cluster E, however, but not for Cluster F, abandonment or desertion was also present. For Cluster F, but not for Cluster E, unwillingness or inability to assume care (out-of-wedlock births) was present.

Cluster G: Underlying feelings of nervousness and worry and a predominant feeling of anger toward the agency characterized this cluster. Significantly absent were feelings of shame, guilt, thankfulness, or numbness. No ethnic group or socioeconomic status constituted a disproportionate share of this cluster. Neglect or abuse of the child was the primary reason for placement, with the Court rather than the Bureau of Child Welfare having jurisdiction of the cases at entry. The children were young, under six years, and inclined to leave placement within a year of entering. The mothers in this cluster saw placement as having been not at all necessary. They considered placement agencies to be usurpers of parental rights and they scored high on the scale of alienation.

Cluster H: The feelings expressed in this last cluster include relief, thankfulness, emptiness, worry, and nervousness. Shame and guilt are significantly absent. The ethnic and socioeconomic composition of this cluster does not differ considerably from the distribution of the total sample. Physical illness of the child-caring person and unwillingness or inability to continue care were the primary reasons for placement. The Bureau of Child Welfare generally had jurisdiction over the case at entry, and the mothers tended to see placement as absolutely or very necessary.

DESCRIPTION OF FATHER CLUSTERS. A separate cluster analysis was undertaken in order to study the patterns of feeling responses of the interviewed fathers. Seven groups of fathers were identified. Four of these included from 17 to 48 fathers, and these clusters are related to nine descriptive variables in Chart II which parallels the chart on mother feelings. Three clusters of fathers, each of which contained only seven cases, have been excluded from the chart because of the smallness of the sample, but their particular configurations are discussed in the text.

Cluster A: The predominant feelings of the fathers in Cluster A were anger, bitterness, and shame. Significantly absent were feelings of emptiness, nervousness, and worry. These men were predominantly white and within the relatively high socioeconomic range of study families. Their children entered placement primarily because the person who was caring for them was unwilling or unable to continue care. The fathers did not think that placement was at all necessary. Their placed children were very young, infants under two years of age, and did not tend to remain in placement a full year.

Cluster B: The fathers in this cluster primarily felt nervousness and worry on the day of placement. Feelings of emptiness and shame were significantly absent. Puerto Rican fathers of low socioeconomic status made up the largest part of this cluster. Placement occurred most frequently because of the mental illness of the child-caring person. The placed children tended to be between two and six years of age.

CHART 2

Father Cluster Groups: Feelings and Descriptive Variables

| Cluster group | Feelings placement day [a] | | Predominant ethnic group | Socioeconomic level | Primary reasons for placement |
	Predominant feelings [c]	Feelings significantly absent [c]			
A (N = 28)	Angry Bitter Ashamed	Empty Nervous Worried	White	High [c]	Unwillingness or inability to continue care
B (N = 23)	Nervous Worried	Empty Ashamed	Puerto Rican [c]	Low [c]	Mental illness
C (N = 17)	Relieved Thankful	Angry Bitter Nervous Worried Ashamed Guilty	—	—	Child behavior [c] Abandonment or desertion
D (N = 48)	Empty Nervous Worried Ashamed Numb	—	—	Middle [c]	Physical illness

[a] Significant differences in feelings for Groups A through D were determined by comparing them with the total sample.

[b] Descriptive variables when footnoted are statistically significant as noted below. Where they are not footnoted the proportion of cases in the category in the cluster is at least one third greater than the proportion of cases in the category in the total sample.

Cluster C: Relief and thankfulness were the predominant feelings of the fathers in Cluster C. Absent were feelings of anger, bitterness, nervousness, worry, shame, or guilt. The ethnic and socioeconomic composition of this group did not differ substantially from the distribution of those variables for the total sample of interviewed fathers. Placement occurred primarily because of the child's behavior or be-

| | Descriptive variables relevant to cluster groups[b] | | | | |
Fathers' opinion of necessity of placement	Jurisdiction of case	Age of child at placement	Child in placement at least one year	Alienation score	Predominant agency attitude
Not at all[c]	—	Under 2[c]	No	—	—
—	—	2 to under 6	—	—	—
absolutely	—	6 or more[c]	—	—	Facilitator[d] Surrogate
—	—	2 to under 6	—	High	—

[c] Significant difference from total sample at $P \leqslant .05$ using Chi square with Yates continuity correction.
[d] Significant difference from total sample at $.05 < P \leqslant .10$ using Chi square with Yates continuity correction.

cause of abandonment or desertion and was frequently seen as having been absolutely necessary. The children of these men were relatively older as a group, six years old or more. Placement agencies were perceived as facilitators of child care and as surrogate parents.

Cluster D: The feelings expressed in this father cluster include emptiness, nervousness, worry, shame, and numbness. No feelings were significantly absent. No ethnic group predominated in this cluster, and the cluster members were mainly at the middle socioeconomic level. Physical illness of the child-caring person was the main reason the children entered placement. The children were predominantly between two and six years of age.

Only one of the four father clusters seems to be similar to any of the mother clusters in any substantial way. Father Cluster C is in many ways comparable to Mother Cluster A. Those two clusters had almost identical feeling patterns on the day of placement, child behavior was a common primary reason for placement in both groups, and both tended to see placement as having been absolutely necessary.

As noted, there were three groups of fathers isolated by the clustering procedure with only seven cases in each. Two of these small clusters were so distinct they are of interest in characterizing special types of reaction patterns. Both clusters were made up predominantly of black men. The primary reason for placement in one group was unwillingness or inability to assume care of the child (usually referring to out-of-wedlock births). Emptiness was the main feeling expressed by those men, with nervousness and thankfulness significantly absent. The children were generally under two years of age, as would be expected considering the predominant reason for placement. The men thought that placement was only somewhat necessary. The second group of seven fathers reported anger to be their predominant feeling on the day of placement. Feelings of relief, emptiness, thankfulness, nervousness, or bitterness were significantly absent. Neglect or abuse was the primary reason for placement of the children of these men, and the Court had jurisdiction of the cases on the day of entry into care.

INTERPRETATION OF CLUSTER ANALYSES. Cluster analysis of the feelings data does not lead to clearcut identification of a feeling typology. Both the concept and the method are complicated and the outcome needs careful and concentrated study. The technique used, however, enables identification of internal subgroups within the total sample which hold together and represent significantly different feeling patterns.

An interesting aspect of the cluster analysis is that not only the presence but also the absence of a feeling can be meaningful. Furthermore, feelings may co-vary in a variety of ways, with associated differences in other descriptive variables. In the data on mothers, for example, Cluster A had as predominant feelings relief and thankfulness; Cluster B had worry and thankfulness. With regard to ethnic group identification, it is then seen that the relief and thankfulness cluster is made up predominantly of white mothers, whereas the group expressing worry and thankfulness is composed predominantly of Puerto Rican mothers. Another example reflects significant absence of feelings. The feelings of the two mother Clusters E and F, both of which are made up predominantly of black women, tended to be fairly similar. In one group, however, thankfulness was significantly absent, whereas in the other group anger and bitterness were significantly absent. The group lacking thankfulness tended to come from a middle-level socioeconomic group, and they were high on the alienation score. They also expressed the feeling that placement was not at all necessary, although the cases included many abandoned and deserted children. The second group of black mothers, without anger or bitterness, were low on the socioeconomic scale, middle on alienation, and they tended to take their children home before the end of the year, although initially they showed inability or unwillingness to assume care.

In the father clusters the presence or absence of certain feelings was associated with several descriptive variables. Shame was significant in Cluster A, together with bitterness and anger, whereas nervousness and worry were significantly absent. This cluster was predominantly white and had the highest socioeconomic level in the sample. The children were predominantly infants, and many fathers expressed the opinion that placement was not at all necessary. In Cluster B, nervousness and worry were significantly present but shame was absent. This cluster was predominantly Puerto Rican, of the lowest socioeconomic level, and mainly had children from ages two to six in placement.

Two conclusions may be drawn. One is that it is impossible to stereotype feeling responses in terms of ethnic group. White, black, and Puerto Rican parents each fell into a variety of clusters characterized by a range of associated factors, such as reason for placement, feelings, status, and attitudes. Furthermore, it is also impossible to identify each cluster with a single dominant variable among the various descriptive variables. A combination of factors and a complex mix appear to be involved in making specific identifications to relate patterns of feelings to the other variables. Certain feelings in combination with others tend to be associated with certain ethnic groups; these in turn are related to various reasons for placement, and they are also associated with age of child at placement, alienation of parents, and responses on the necessity of placement. Although cluster analysis technique, as already noted, did not provide all the answers, it proved to be a useful method of looking at the nature of filial deprivation and relating feelings to other variables associated with placement.

IMPLICATIONS OF FEELING ANALYSIS

The investigation of feelings of parents when children are placed was undertaken as one aspect of the study of filial deprivation. Expressed feelings cannot, of course, be assumed to represent the whole picture; they may reflect what the respondent wishes the investigator to hear, or they may be a superficial expression which avoids deeper reactions and denies underlying emotions. Taken at face value, however, and recognizing the limitations, they do represent self reports by parents in connection with what is generally a crisis period, when children have left home. The various analytic techniques applied in order to study the nature and direction of these expressed feelings, their factor components, and the clustering of the parents with regard to them suggest that identifiable feeling patterns exist, and that feeling clusters relate significantly to a series of descriptive variables.

The exploration of the feeling data began with a review of the literature on both animal and human behavior with regard to filial separation. The social work literature was sparse, not systematic, and not at all enlightening in explaining or even describing what happens to parents when children enter care. The particular feelings selected for study were derived from pilot interviews with non-study parents of children in placement. The family instrument incorporated both checklist and open-ended questions on feelings, and responses were obtained from both mothers and fathers of children in care.

Family interview data indicated substantial concentration in certain feeling areas, in particular, sadness and worry; moderate occurrence of feelings such as nervousness, anger, bitterness, thankfulness, and relief; and other less frequent but important feeling components such as guilt and shame. Mothers and fathers tended to report comparable feelings, with some differences in emphasis.

The analysis of feeling referents was of particular interest in that it showed the importance of looking at the direction and object of the feeling. Thus anger tended to be interpersonal, rather than antisociety; guilt was self-directed; worry tended to be about the child. Knowledge of both feelings and referents is essential to an understanding of parental reactions, and as a base for working with families. Furthermore, the fact that a wide range of socioeconomic and demographic variables relate to combinations of particular feelings and referents is an indication of the complexity of the relationships among environmental circumstances, social problems, and emotional life.

Two major statistical techniques were applied to the feelings data to organize and reduce the multitude of information into comprehensible patterns. Factor analysis helped clarify the main dimensions underlying the intercorrelations among the feeling-referent combinations. Among those identified were the factors labeled as interpersonal hostility, self-denigration, agency hostility, self-involvement, and shame coupled with relief. On the whole mothers tended to be heavily self-involved and typically focused on their own problems rather than the child's in relation to the placement situation. They also showed substantial hostility to other persons as well as to the agencies. Fathers expressed strong guilt and shame, were less self-involved and more child oriented.

These findings threw light on the underlying structure of the feelings and referents but did not answer, except tangentially, the complicated question of whether the individuals involved tended to form clusters with characteristic patterns of feelings. To accomplish this, the technique of cluster analysis was utilized. This method compared individual reaction patterns and identified groups of mothers and groups of fathers who clustered in terms of similar parental feeling syndromes. These have been described in some detail in the chapter and the charts indicate mother clusters and father clusters with associated descriptive variables. The findings show the fallacy of expecting to find a single critical variable, and point up the need to look at the overall feeling patterns and relate them to a range of descriptive variables.

The findings presented in this chapter can be utilized in a variety of ways. Further study of the complicated emotional reactions of parents when children enter care will help deepen understanding of the consequences of filial deprivation. Insights into such reaction patterns will be useful in developing work with parents, so that opportunities for extending help can be identified and so that there can be a differential approach to mothers and fathers whose children have entered care. The parent who has strong feelings of anger and alienation represents a different kind of person and family than the one who is relieved and thankful, although sad. The exploration of feelings while children are in care, and the recognition on the part of parents of their own feelings toward placement, may contribute positively to the possible return of the child home. It may also be preventive in the sense of making for better overall family adjustment and avoiding the all too frequent reentry of the returned child into care. The concern with the parent, furthermore, emphasizes that the focus in foster care cannot be only the child; the family is deeply involved—before, during, and after placement—and needs to be part of the treatment picture. The separation of child and parent cuts two ways—the child is separated from the parent, but the parent is also separated from the child.

CHAPTER FIVE

Parental Attitudes and
Expectations

ALTHOUGH attitudes are not always predictive of behavior, they do provide clues to motivations underlying actions. Where a substantial number of families have experienced a crisis such as placement of children, and where there are extensive background data on each case, the social attitudes of the parents are of particular interest, since they may help explain the response patterns of different parents to the common experience.

In the present research attitudes of parents were studied along six main dimensions. The most generalized dimension was that of social orientation. More specific to the common experience were attitudes toward foster care agencies. In addition, four aspects of attitudes related to child and family life were studied. These included attitudes regarding child rearing, desirable child traits, goals and aspirations of parents for children, and parental role expectations and performances.

Mothers and fathers of the majority of children in care

have already been described as a poverty population in terms of a number of socioeconomic variables. The general social attitudes of these parents are similar to attitudes of disadvantaged people with limited access to opportunity and money. Attitudes of the study sample toward foster care agencies with whom they have been involved, however, do not necessarily correspond to their generalized social attitudes. It may be hypothesized that the direct experience of the placement process, the dependence on the foster care agency, and the personal interaction with the social work staff are factors which would tend to lead to a far more positive attitude on the part of these parents toward agencies than would be anticipated from their alienation stance toward society in general. On the other hand, one would expect that those aspects of the attitude survey which relate to family and child life could be compatible with the basic social class variables already described. Study families tend toward an authoritarian view of child rearing; they also prefer child traits shown in other studies to have been chosen by lower class groups; and they tend basically to associate themselves, as mothers and fathers, with traditional sex roles in family life.

Basic to the analysis which follows is the study of associations between the attitude data and the socioeconomic data, and, where appropriate, between such key variables in the study as reason for placement and parental feelings. Intra-attitudinal analyses are also presented. One of the goals of the attitude survey was to compare the study population with other groups, some similar and some dissimilar in background. For this reason, wherever appropriate, comparative data from other relevant investigations are reported.

GENERALIZED SOCIAL ATTITUDES

In order to obtain measures of the social orientation of parents of placed children, responses were sought along three dimensions. These were (1) alienation; (2) calculativeness; and (3) trust. The items utilized to measure each dimension had been developed and in some cases standardized in other research studies, and were selected so that comparative data could be reported. The major scale used in this area was the five-item anomia index developed by Srole to measure alienation.[1] In addition, items from the work of Struening and Richardson were utilized to measure calculativeness and trust.[2] The correlation between the scores on calculativeness and alienation was significant at .35. There are also low but significant negative correlations between trust and calculativeness, and trust and alienation.

ALIENATION. The concept of alienation is typically used with reference to a sense of futility, friendlessness, pessimism, impotence. The use of the term in this study is synonomous with the concept of "anomie" or "anomy," which has a dictionary definition as follows:

1. Leo Srole, "Social Integration and Certain Corollaries, An Exploratory Study," *American Sociological Review,* XXI (1956), pp. 706–16. Permission to utilize these items was obtained in correspondence with the author, who utilizes the term "anomia" to describe his formulation of the concept.
2. Elmer L. Struening and Arthur H. Richardson, "A Factor Analytic Exploration of the Alienation, Anomia and Authoritarian Domain," *American Sociological Review,* XXX (1965), pp. 770–76. Permission to utilize these items was obtained in correspondence with Dr. Struening.

A state of society in which normative standards of conduct and belief are weak or lacking; also: a similar condition in an individual commonly characterized by disorientation, anxiety, and isolation.[3]

In a classic article entitled "On the Meaning of Alienation" Seeman reviews and summarizes the work done by social scientists on this concept.[4] He makes explicit the many meanings implicit in the usages of the term, especially noting the following: (a) a sense of powerlessness, or the belief that one's behavior does not contribute to the determination of outcomes; (b) a sense of normlessness, or the felt lack of personally relevant rules governing behavior; (c) a sense of isolation, or detachment from others, lack of involvement or a sense of belonging; (d) a sense of meaninglessness, or the absence of a world view in which one believes; and (e) a sense of self-estrangement, or an objectification of self, a sense of foreignness of self to self.

A widely utilized scale to obtain a measure of the concept encompassing those meanings is the index created by Srole. The five items he includes, which were incorporated in the field interview for the present study, are the following:

1. These days a person doesn't really know who he can count on.

2. In spite of what people say, the lot of the average man is getting worse, not better.

3. *Webster's Seventh New Collegiate Dictionary* (G. & C. Merriam, Springfield, Massachusetts, 1965, p. 37).

4. Melvin Seeman, "On the Meaning of Alienation," *American Sociological Review*, XXIV (1959), pp. 783–91.

3. Most public officials are not really interested in the problems of the average man.

4. Nowadays, a person has to live pretty much for today and let tomorrow take care of itself.

5. It's hardly fair to bring children into the world the way things look for the future.

In terms of scoring, the greater the number of items agreed with, the greater the degree of alienation, or as Srole terms it "anomia." The range of scores goes from zero through five, zero indicating agreement with none of the items, five indicating agreement with all of them.

In 1956 Srole indicated that there was evidence that anomia is inversely related to socioeconomic status.[5] This has been supported in further research utilizing the Srole items.[6] Studies have also ascertained that many other variables are systematically related to anomia, e.g., age, sex, marital status, rural residence, and aspirations. A number of hypotheses have been proposed to explain the substantial body of data collected in applications of the scale.

In 1959 Meier and Bell, on the basis of their study of the relationships between anomia and factors such as age, income, education, class identification, marital status, and religion, concluded that "Socially structured limitations to access to the means for the achievement of life goals produce

5. Srole, "Social Integration."
6. See, for example, Ephraim H. Mizruchi, "Social Structure and Anomia," *American Sociological Review,* XXV (1960), pp. 645–54; Richard L. Simpson and Max H. Miller, "Social Status and Anomia," *Social Problems,* X (1963), pp. 256–64; Thomas S. Langner and Stanley T. Michael, *Life Stress and Mental Health* (New York, Free Press, 1963).

anomia in the individuals so affected." [7] In a similar vein Rhodes in 1964 interpreted his study findings with the comment, "These data . . . tempt one to suggest that anomia is maximized where distance between aspirations and life chances for success is maximized. . . ." [8] McClosky and Schaar, in 1965, summed up a widely accepted interpretation of the various findings with regard to anomia:

Investigators who have administered the Srole scale to various samples have uniformly reported that anomy is highest among certain sectors of the population: old people, the widowed, the divorced and separated, persons of low education, those with low incomes and low prestige occupations, people experiencing downward social mobility, Negroes, and foreign born, farmers and other rural residents. . . .

All the groups just mentioned have one thing in common: they are outside the articulate, prosperous, and successful sectors of the population.[9]

The findings of the present study are consistent with this interpretation. In general the parents in this study are characterized by relatively high alienation scores. Furthermore, the alienation scores were significantly associated with both socioeconomic status and ethnic group. Members of the relatively high socioeconomic level in the study, and the ethnic group with the easiest access to opportunity for achievement, tended to show less alienation from society, as seen in Table V.1.

7. Dorothy L. Meier and Wendall Bell, "Anomia and Differential Access to the Achievement of Life Goals," *American Sociological Review*, XXIV (1959), pp. 189–202.
8. Lewis Rhodes, "Anomia, Aspiration and Status," *Social Forces*, XLII (1964), p. 439.
9. Herbert McClosky and John H. Schaar, "Psychological Dimensions of Anomy," *American Sociological Review*, XXX (1965), p. 19.

TABLE V.1

Mean Alienation Scores[a] of Mothers and Fathers
by Ethnic Group and Socioeconomic Level

	Mothers $(N = 297)$	*Fathers* $(N = 137)$
Ethnic group		
White	2.21	1.96
Black	2.98	3.22
Puerto Rican	3.09	2.69
Socioeconomic level		
High	2.25	2.32
Middle	3.06	2.64
Low	3.11	2.86
Total	*2.81*	*2.61*

[a] Scores based on number of items agreed with of five
presented.

On the average, study parents agreed with over half of
the items, mothers showing somewhat higher alienation
than fathers. White men and women were significantly less
alienated than black or Puerto Rican men and women. Indeed, the highest mean score for alienation was that of
black fathers, who were significantly higher in alienation
than either white or Puerto Rican fathers.

The particular subgroups within the mother and father
groups where significant differences were found on alienation scores are as follows: [10]

MOTHERS	*FATHERS*
White vs. Black	White vs. Black
White vs. Puerto Rican	White vs. Puerto Rican

10. Significant at $P \leq .05$ level, based on application of t-tests.

High vs. low socio-	Black vs. Puerto Rican
economic	High vs. low socio-
level	economic
High vs. middle socio-	level
economic	
level	

These differences in alienation scores within the study sample support the findings generally reported in the literature: that alienation, as measured by the Srole anomia scale, tends to be associated with the inarticulate, the poor, and the unsuccessful sectors of the population. In addition to the findings within the study sample, this is further reinforced by comparing the scores of this study sample with those of other populations where the Srole scale has been applied.

A study by Reeder and Reeder of wed and unwed Los Angeles white, black, and Mexican-American mothers attending prenatal clinics is of interest.[11] The women in the Reeders' study were considered to be "urban poor" since the annual income of 80 percent of their sample was under $4,000. The mean alienation score of Reeders' sample matched that of the present study almost exactly.[12] Furthermore the Reeders reported lower scores for white women than for Mexican-American or black women.

Two other studies in which the study samples were from generally better economic circumstances showed average alienation scores that were much lower than those obtained

11. Leo G. Reeder and Sharon J. Reeder, "Social Isolation and Illegitimacy," *Journal of Marriage and the Family,* XXXI (August 1969), pp. 451–61.
12. When the anomia scores were scaled differently from the present study, comparability was approximated through the use of ratio estimates.

in the present research. These are Srole's research on white transit riders in Springfield, Massachusetts,[13] and Mizruchi's study of heads of households in a small city in upstate New York.[14]

In general it may be concluded that the degree of alienation in the parents of children in foster care, as measured by the Srole scale, corresponds to the level of alienation shown by other populations in similar socioeconomic circumstances, being substantially higher than that of more advantaged groups. Socioeconomic circumstances appear to be a relevant correlate of alienation for groups with and without children in placement.

TRUST. An attitude of trust represents a social orientation almost directly antithetical to alienation. Five items from the work of Struening and Richardson [15] were utilized to measure this attitude. The larger the number of items agreed with, the more trusting the attitude was considered to be. The following five items were presented to respondents for agreement or disagreement:

1. It is easy to get along with people.
2. People will be honest with you as long as you are honest with them.
3. Considering everything that is going on today, things look bright for the younger generation.
4. In spite of the fast pace of modern living, it is easy to have many close friends that you can really count on.
5. Most people can be trusted.

13. Srole, "Social Integration."
14. Ephraim H. Mizruchi, "Social Structure and Anomia," *American Sociological Review*, XXV (October 1960), pp. 645–54.
15. Struening and Richardson, "A Factor Analytic Exploration."

TABLE V.2

Mean Trust Scores[a] of Mothers and Fathers
by Ethnic Group and Socioeconomic Level

	Mothers (N = 297)	*Fathers* (N = 137)
Ethnic group		
White	2.75	2.98
Black	2.88	2.80
Puerto Rican	2.24	2.78
Socioeconomic level		
High	2.51	2.66
Middle	2.73	3.02
Low	2.71	2.88
Total	*2.64*	*2.85*

[a] Scores based on number of items agreed with of five
presented.

As seen in Table V.2 both mothers and fathers agreed, on the average, with about half of these items, with fathers agreeing slightly more frequently than mothers. Puerto Rican mothers were significantly less trusting than either white or black mothers. This was not the case with fathers, who differed little among themselves by ethnic group. Although the differences were not statistically significant, it is interesting that both mothers and fathers of the high socioeconomic level in the study tended to be somewhat less trusting than did their counterparts of middle or low socioeconomic status.

There were relatively few significant differences among subgroups on the trust dimension as compared with alienation. Such differences appeared only between mothers in the following groups: Puerto Rican vs. white and Puerto

Rican vs. black. Trust scores were relatively low for Puerto Rican mothers but were also paradoxically low for the higher socioeconomic level. The trust items did not appear to be related in such a consistent fashion to ethnic group or economic status as were the alienation scores.

CALCULATIVENESS. Just as there was some ambiguity with regard to the trust dimension, there was ambiguity with calculativeness. The five items selected to measure an attitude of calculativeness, also based on the work of Struening and Richardson,[16] were in general strongly agreed with by all study subgroups. The items were as follows:

1. A man should be allowed to make as much money as he can.
2. In a society where almost everyone is out for himself, people soon come to distrust each other.
3. People will do almost anything if the reward is high enough.
4. Too many people in our society are just out for themselves and don't really care for anyone else.
5. It is usually best to tell your superiors or bosses what they really want to hear.

Of the items presented, both mothers and fathers agreed on the average with just under four of the five statements. Table V.3 shows the responses of the sample subgroups.

White parents of both sexes were significantly lower with regard to calculativeness than were Puerto Rican parents. White mothers were lower in calculativeness than black

16. *Ibid.*

TABLE V.3

Mean Calculativeness Scores[a] of Mothers and Fathers
by Ethnic Group and Socioeconomic Level

	Mothers (N = 297)	*Fathers* (N = 137)
Ethnic group		
White	3.41	3.66
Black	3.90	3.96
Puerto Rican	3.76	4.22
Socioeconomic level		
High	3.53	3.82
Middle	3.82	4.00
Low	3.79	4.00
Total	*3.73*	*3.94*

[a] Scores based on number of items agreed with of five
presented.

mothers. No significant differences between socioeconomic
levels were found for either mothers or fathers.

Analysis of responses on both trust and calculativeness is
limited to the present sample, since these scales have not
been standardized on large populations, and the comparative data available for the alienation variable do not exist
for the other scales. Thus, no conclusion can be drawn as
to whether the generally high calculativeness orientation is
unique to the present sample or would be found in comparable populations.

ATTITUDES TOWARD AGENCIES

All the parents interviewed in the study sample were aware
that their children were in foster care. An important ques-

tion for practice is to learn how such parents perceive the agency function. Knowledge of parental attitudes toward agencies can affect ways of working with natural parents while children are in care, as well as planning for return of the children when this is appropriate. It was hypothesized that parents might see the child welfare agency as fulfilling primarily one of the three following roles: (1) facilitators of child care, helping families in time of need; (2) usurpers of parental rights, taking over child care; or (3) surrogates for parents, fulfilling a socially appropriate role.

The relationships between these three types of attitudes toward agencies and the social orientation of parents along the dimensions of alienation, trust, and calculativeness was explored. The three social attitudes were hypothesized as being associated with agency attitudes in the following ways: parents with a trusting orientation would be expected to be more likely to see agencies as facilitating family life; parents highly alienated from society should tend to see agencies as usurping their rights; and parents with a strong calculativeness orientation should be more ready to accept agencies as surrogate caretakers.

The agency attitude scales developed for the present study had a twofold purpose. They were intended primarily to secure descriptive data on parental reactions, which could then be analyzed against the other characteristics of the sample, such as demographic information and reason for placement. Second, the scales were designed to test the hypotheses mentioned above regarding the relationships between generalized social attitudes and specific agency attitudes.

The first step in the development of the agency attitude scale was the formulation of thirty items, ten on each dimension. These items were derived from a pilot study in which parents of children in care (not in the study sample) were asked a range of open-ended questions about attitudes toward agencies. The original thirty items were subsequently reduced to nine, three on each dimension, by eliminating ambiguous items with low content validity.[17]

The items included in the final scale are as follows:

Facilitator items

1. It's a good thing there are institutions and foster mothers to do the job when a real mother is not able to take care of her child.

2. If not for the agency helping with the children many mothers would go to pieces in time of trouble.

3. When a family can't manage a child, an agency can take over until he behaves better and is ready to come home.

Usurper items

1. Agencies act like parents have no rights at all—they think they own the children.

2. If agencies would leave parents alone, they could manage their own children.

3. There must be something in it for agencies, the way they break up families.

---

17. The reduction procedure was done in two steps. First, 35 social workers judged the content validity of the original items. The four items on each dimension judged to be the least representative of assigned attitudes were eliminated. Of the remaining six items on each dimension, the three with the lowest average deviation from that dimension's mean, based on the pretest responses, were selected for the final agency attitude scale.

Surrogate items

1. Just because you give birth to a child doesn't mean you have all the responsibility of bringing him up—the state should take some responsibility too.

2. Children are better off in institutions; they know better how to bring them up.

3. When you come right down to it, the children belong to the government, so why shouldn't they take care of them?

The scales were not conceived to be measuring attitudes which are necessarily mutually exclusive. It is possible, for example, for parents to have ambivalent or mixed reactions to the agency, just as they showed varying patterns of feelings about their children entering care. The purpose was to see if there were certain main thrusts of parental agency attitudes and then to relate these to overall social attitudes as well as other demographic and placement variables.

Since each parent could agree with from none of the items on each dimension to all three of them, the range of each scale was from zero to 3. The results, however, were highly skewed. Both mothers and fathers appeared to see agencies as facilitators rather than as usurpers or surrogates. Mothers and fathers agreed, on the average, with 2.6 of the 3 facilitator items, whereas both parents agreed with an average of only 0.6 usurper and 0.4 surrogate items. Responses on the three dimensions of agency attitudes tested are shown in Table V.4. In addition to the subsample analysis by ethnic group and socioeconomic level, responses were also analyzed by religion and case jurisdiction. This was considered important because of the relationship of

TABLE V.4

Mean Agency Attitude Scores[a] of Mothers and Fathers by
Ethnic Group, Religion, Socioeconomic Level, and
Case Jurisdiction at Entry

	Mothers (N = 297)			Fathers (N = 137)		
	Facili-tator	Usurper	Surro-gate	Facili-tator	Usurper	Surro-gate
Ethnic group						
White	2.7	0.5	0.3	2.4	0.5	0.2
Black	2.6	0.8	0.3	2.6	0.7	0.2
Puerto Rican	2.7	0.8	0.7	2.8	0.7	0.9
Religion						
Catholic	2.6	0.7	0.5	2.6	0.6	0.6
Protestant	2.6	0.8	0.3	2.7	0.7	0.2
Jewish	2.8	0.3	0.2	2.5	0.5	0.3
Socioeconomic level						
High	2.7	0.5	0.2	2.6	0.5	0.3
Middle	2.7	0.6	0.3	2.7	0.6	0.5
Low	2.5	0.9	0.5	2.6	0.8	0.5
Case jurisdiction						
Court	2.5	1.1	0.5	2.9	1.0	0.7
Bureau of Child Welfare	2.7	0.6	0.4	2.6	0.6	0.3
Total	2.6	0.7	0.4	2.6	0.6	0.4

[a] Each category included three items, and the score was based on the average number of items agreed with in each category.

these latter factors to the pattern of agency service in New York. In addition to the fact that a child, at the time of the study, might enter placement under the jurisdiction of either the Bureau of Child Welfare or the Family Court, statutory provisions specified that, whenever feasible, a child should be placed with an agency that has the same religious orientation as that of the family.

Although the major findings here are the high facilitator as compared to low usurper and surrogate scores, there are also some significant differences in the subgroups. Whites and Jewish mothers and fathers tended to see the agencies as usurpers less than non-whites, Catholics, or Protestants. Seeing the agency as a surrogate was most characteristic of Puerto Rican parents. Seeing the agency as a facilitator was comparable in all economic groups. Neither mothers nor fathers who maintained usurper or surrogate orientations tended to be at the highest socioeconomic level.

Perhaps the analysis most relevant to this line of investigation is case jurisdiction. Parents with children placed under the jurisdiction of the Bureau of Child Welfare were more likely to hold a facilitator attitude than those with children placed under Court jurisdiction. Those with children placed through the Court were more likely to agree with usurper items than those with children placed by the Bureau of Child Welfare. This is not an unexpected finding, since the Court cases are frequently associated with neglect and abuse, or some aspect of parental incompetence, and parents are resentful of the interference of authorities.

Utilizing t-tests, differences between means were significant at $P \leqslant .05$ level for the following subgroups:

MOTHERS	*FATHERS*

Facilitator attitude

High vs. low socio-
     economic
     level
	White vs. Puerto Ricans

Court vs. BCW
     jurisdiction
	Court vs. BCW
	     jurisdiction

Usurper attitude

White vs. Black White vs. Puerto Rican Jewish vs. Catholic Jewish vs. Protestant	

High vs. low socio-
     economic
     level
	High vs. low socio-
	     economic
	     level

Court vs. BCW
     jurisdiction
	Court vs. BCW
	     jurisdiction

Surrogate attitude

Puerto Rican vs. White Puerto Rican vs. Black	Puerto Rican vs. White Puerto Rican vs. Black Catholic vs. Protestant

High vs. low socio-
     economic
     level	

The analysis of agency attitudes indicates that the parents generally tended to see the agency as a facilitator rather than a usurper or surrogate. However, within subgroups Puerto Rican parents tended to have higher scores on the surrogate dimension, and case jurisdiction was found to be related to differences in the usurper attitude.

The hypotheses relating agency attitudes to general social attitudes were only partially substantiated. The first pair of attitudes compared—social orientation of trust in relation to facilitator attitude toward agencies—did not show a significant relationship for either mothers or fathers. This may have been due, in part, to the strong extent to which the facilitator position was held by most of the study sample. The second pair studied—social orientation of alienation in relation to usurper attitude toward agencies—did prove to have a low but significant correlation of .29 for mothers and .37 for fathers. The third pair examined—social orientation of calculativeness in relation to agency attitude of surrogate—also showed significant correlations, but at a very low level, .12 for mothers and .19 for fathers.

In the face of such low correlations there are few definitive conclusions to be drawn. The strongest relationship was found between alienation as a social attitude and the perception of the agency as a usurper of parental rights. For the sample as a whole, however, alienation was more pervasive than the usurper position, and the extent to which parents saw agencies as facilitators was far more general than had been anticipated. The major finding is that general social orientations of parents are not highly related to attitudes to foster care agencies along the suggested dimensions. Social attitudes are "class and caste" oriented, whereas the specific placement experience appears to be more related to the parental attitudes toward agencies.

ATTITUDES TOWARD CHILDREN

The investigation of the general social orientation of the parents was followed by a study of their attitudes toward children. Three areas were explored. These were (1) author-itarian-permissive approaches to child rearing; (2) parental preferences with regard to child character traits; and (3) educational and occupational expectations for children on the part of parents. Where appropriate, instruments developed in other studies were used, so that comparisons could be made with findings on other populations.

AUTHORITARIAN-PERMISSIVE DIMENSION IN CHILD REARING. An area of concern in child-rearing studies is whether parents approach their task with a generally authoritarian or a generally permissive orientation.

Although no single instrument found in the literature appeared to be appropriate in its entirety for the present study, several items contained in an investigation of personality patterns in women by Loevinger were relevant to exploration of authoritarian-permissive patterns of child rearing.[18] Pairs of items were presented to the respondent, each offering them a socially acceptable but alternative position on specific aspects of behavior. Respondents were asked to choose the one item in each pair which most closely approximated their attitude toward that behavior. The following six paired items representing the dimension of authoritarianism-permissiveness toward children were utilized in the present study. The letter designation after each item in-

18. Jane Loevinger, "Measuring Personality Patterns in Women," *Genetic Psychology Monograph*, LXV (1962), pp. 53–136. Permission to use these items was obtained in correspondence with Dr. Loevinger. For a discussion of the problems involved in measuring personality traits see Jane Loevinger, "Measurement in Clinical Research," in *Handbook of Clinical Psychology*, ed. B. Wolman (New York, McGraw-Hill, 1965), pp. 78–94.

dicates whether it was considered by the investigator to represent an authoritarian (A) or permissive (P) approach. This designation was not, of course, revealed to respondents.

Hitting

No child should be allowed to hit his mother. (A)
A mother should not be hard with a small child who strikes her. (P)

Hating

Most children have times when they hate their mothers. (P)
There is something wrong with a child who hates his mother. (A)

Lying

It is fun to hear a five-year-old tell big stories. (P)
A five-year-old should be taught not to tell big stories that aren't true. (A)

Crying

You can spoil a tiny baby by picking him up every time he cries. (A)
You cannot spoil a tiny baby by picking him up every time he cries. (P)

Talking back

Children should be allowed to talk back to their parents. (P)
Children should not be fresh to their parents. (A)

Wetting

A three-year-old who wets his pants should be made
to feel ashamed of himself. (A)

There is no use making a child feel ashamed when he
wets his pants. (P)

The highest number of authoritarian choices a parent
could make was six. The same was true for permissive
choices. Most often respondents "split their vote," making
some authoritarian and some permissive choices. Generally
parents in the study tended toward authoritarianism as
compared with permissiveness in their attitudes toward
child rearing. The average score for mothers and fathers
was 3.9 for authoritarianism, with the complementary
score for permissiveness being 2.1. There were revealing
differences, however, in responses to the various items.

A large majority of parents (ranging from two-thirds to
nine-tenths), selected the authoritarian positions of not allowing a child to talk back, not approving lying or telling
"big stories," not allowing a child ever to hit his mother,
and not picking a baby up every time he cries. Half of the
parents felt there is something wrong with a child who
hates his mother. The only area where a generally permissive parental reaction was secured was on toilet training.
Two-thirds of both mothers and fathers considered it to be
useless to make a child who "wets his pants" feel ashamed.

How do these findings relate to other studies, and what
do they tell us about the parents whose children enter care?
Any comparisons with normative data must take into account the changing patterns of child rearing in the last several decades. Furthermore, parental attitudes have changed
in different ways for different social classes. There are a

number of studies in the literature which illustrate these changes in attitudes.

Studies done in the 1940s tended to find lower-class mothers more permissive than their middle-class counterparts. The work of Davis and Havighurst [19] found lower-class parents more permissive in training, whereas middle-class parents insisted on a stricter regime for their children and generally sought to be more controlling of their children's impulses. Investigations in the fifties, however, literally found the opposite to be the case. Studies by Sears, Maccoby, and Levin [20] and White,[21] indicated greater permissiveness on the part of women of higher socioeconomic status than on the part of lower-class women. Findings of this kind continued into the sixties. The disadvantaged mothers studied by Radin and Kamii,[22] when compared to middle-class women, tended to have much more overprotective, suppressive, and authoritarian attitudes about child rearing.

Comparisons among attitude investigations are generally limited because of differences in characteristics of populations studied, as well as in instruments used. Thus generalizations are difficult. In the present study, there were a number of interesting relationships between degree of authoritari-

19. Allison Davis and Robert J. Havighurst, "Social Class and Color Differences in Child Rearing," *American Sociological Review,* XI (1946), p. 710.

20. Robert R. Sears, Eleanor E. Maccoby, and Harry Levin, *Patterns of Child Rearing* (New York, Row, Peterson, 1957).

21. Martha S. White, "Social Class, Child Rearing Practices and Child Behavior," *American Sociological Review,* XXII (1957), p. 708.

22. Norma Radin and Constance K. Kamii, "The Child-Rearing Attitudes of Disadvantaged Negro Mothers and Some Educational Implications," *Journal of Negro Education,* XXXIV (1965), pp. 138–46.

anism and ethnicity, religion, and socioeconomic level, as shown in Table V.5.

There was negligible difference between middle and low socioeconomic groups in the sample with reference to authoritarianism; differences of the low and middle groups from the high groups were statistically significant for fathers, but not for mothers. When ethnic groups and religious groups were compared significant differences emerged. Based on t-tests, the following differences significant at the

TABLE V.5

Permissive-Authoritarian Child Rearing
Attitudes of Mothers and Fathers by Ethnic Group,
Religion, and Socioeconomic Level

| | Average number of authoritarian items chosen from six paired sets | |
	Mothers (N = 297)	Fathers (N = 137)
Ethnic group		
White	3.4	3.4
Black	4.3	4.2
Puerto Rican	3.8	4.1
Religion		
Catholic	3.8	3.9
Protestant	4.3	4.4
Jewish	3.1	2.6
Socioeconomic level		
High	3.7	3.4
Middle	4.1	4.2
Low	4.0	4.1
Total	*3.9*	*3.9*

.05 level were found, the first-named group being characterized by higher authoritarianism in child-rearing attitudes.

MOTHERS	FATHERS
Black vs. White	Black vs. White
Puerto Rican vs. White	Puerto Rican vs. White
Black vs. Puerto Rican	
Protestant vs. Catholic	Protestant vs. Catholic
Catholic vs. Jewish	Catholic vs. Jewish
Protestant vs. Jewish	Protestant vs. Jewish
	Low vs. high socio-economic level
	Middle vs. high socio-economic level

The fact that ethnic group, religion, and socioeconomic status are significantly interrelated makes it difficult to decide whether one variable is more critical than another. It is apparent, however, that Protestant mothers and fathers tend to hold more authoritarian attitudes than either Catholic or Jewish parents, and Jewish parents exhibited the least authoritarian attitude of all three groups. Furthermore, white parents tend to see child rearing from a less authoritarian perspective than either black or Puerto Rican parents. Finally, black mothers were the most authoritarian of all mothers, differing significantly not only from white, but also from Puerto Rican women in this respect. Although these differences existed between subgroups within the study sample, the study group as a whole tended to have an authoritarian perspective.

CHILD TRAITS PREFERRED BY PARENTS. Parental attitudes as well as values are revealed by their choices of the kinds of traits parents would like their children to possess. Preferences of traits tend to reflect social class position, as shown by Kohn.[23] Data from the Kohn studies were compared with results in the present study sample.

Kohn has conceptualized parental values as "the values that parents would most like to see embodied in their children's behavior—the characteristics they consider most desirable to inculcate in their children." [24] To operationalize this concept he presented parents with a list of 17 characteristics known to be generally valued, and asked them to choose those few they thought were most desirable for 10- or 11-year-old children. Data on parental values utilizing this procedure were gathered by Kohn and his associates from parents in different locales, including Washington, D.C.[25] and Turin, Italy.[26]

Seven of the seventeen child characteristics included by Kohn in his work were incorporated into the present study. The seven traits utilized were those which were most frequently selected by the Washington, D.C. parents. The parents in the present study were asked to choose the three

23. Melvin L. Kohn, *Class and Conformity, A Study in Values* (Illinois, The Dorsey Press, 1969). Also see below.
24. *Ibid.*, p. 18.
25. Melvin L. Kohn, "Social Class and Parental Values," *American Journal of Sociology*, LXIV (1959), pp. 337–51.
26. Leonard I. Pearlin and Melvin L. Kohn, "Social Class, Occupation and Parental Values: A Cross-National Study," *American Sociological Review*, XXIV (1966), pp. 466–79.

traits (from the following seven) which they considered most desirable in a 10-year-old child: (1) honest, (2) happy, (3) considerate, (4) dependable, (5) self-controlled, (6) obedient, (7) neat and clean. Since the list of traits was presented to all parents in the order above, there is a possibility of list bias in results. Analysis of choice showed differentiation by socioeconomic level as well as close correspondence with Kohn's results, both of which support the dependability of the collected data.

TABLE V.6

Traits Chosen as Preferred in a Ten-Year-Old Child
by Mothers and Fathers

	Percent choosing trait as one of three most preferred	
	Mothers (N = 297)	Fathers (N = 137)
Honest	70	74
Happy	57	58
Obedient	53	49
Neat and clean	46	52
Self-controlled	29	26
Considerate	25	23
Dependable	22	18

It is apparent from Table V.6 that one choice, honest, led the field as the trait most preferred by both parents.[27] Three traits followed, each receiving a majority choice: happy, obedient, and neat and clean. Considerate, dependable, and self-controlled were relatively low in level of

27. This was the case not only in the present study, but in the two investigations of Kohn in Washington and in Italy.

TABLE V.7

Social Class of Parents More Frequently Choosing Specified Child Traits in Three Studies

Preferred child trait	Present study		Washington, D.C. study		Italian study	
	Mothers	Fathers	Mothers	Fathers	Mothers	Fathers
Self-controlled	Higher[a]	—	Higher[a]	Higher[a]	Higher[a]	Higher[a]
Considerate	Higher[b]	Higher[b]	Higher[a]	Higher[a]	Higher[a]	—
Happy	Higher[a]	Higher	Higher[a]	Higher	—	Higher[a]
Neat and clean	Lower[a]	Lower[b]	Lower[a]	—	Lower[a]	Lower[b]
Obedient	Lower	Lower[b]	Lower[a]	Lower[a]	Lower[a]	Lower[a]

[a] $P \leqslant .05$ based on the Chi-square test.
[b] $.05 < P \leqslant .20$ based on the Chi-square test.

168

choice. There was close correspondence in the distribution of choices by the mothers and fathers.

The hypothesis that parents' preferences in child traits tend to differ according to socioeconomic level is supported by the data, and these findings reconfirm Kohn's investigations. Before direct comparisons could be made, however, a reclassification of the study sample was necessary to make the socioeconomic categories more comparable to the other studies. The present research used three categories of socioeconomic level, while Kohn's studies had two.

In determining class status in his studies Kohn utilized an index composed of the weighted combination of two variables, occupation and education. Both the upper and lower groups in his samples consisted entirely of intact families with men who had steady jobs. In the present study sample there were few intact families, about half of the families were supported by public assistance, and two-thirds of them had income falling in the "poverty range." For comparative purposes some approximate redivision of families was needed. It was decided that the known income, education, and occupation data would justify identifying the third of the families in the present study with a "high" socioeconomic level with Kohn's higher class (which he called "middle class"). The remaining two-thirds of the study sample would be regarded as roughly comparable to Kohn's lower class (which he called "working class"), although at the lowest level the present study families were actually at a more acute poverty level.

Table V.7 clearly indicates the similarity between the Kohn studies in Washington, D.C. and Italy and the present New York City parent sample on five preferred child traits by social class.[28] The two remaining traits, honest and dependable, were not differentiated by social class and therefore are not included in the table.

"Higher class" parents in all three studies more consistently chose self-control, happiness, and considerateness as preferred traits for a ten-year-old child than did "lower class" parents. Obedience and being neat and clean were traits more frequently chosen by "lower class" parents in all three studies than by "higher class" parents. The overall consistency between the findings of Kohn in his Washington and Italian studies and those of the present research underscores the relationship between socioeconomic circumstances and parental attitudes. These findings were not specifically related to placement of children, but the trends appear to be substantially the same for families whether children were at home or in foster care.

EXPECTATIONS FOR CHILD. The educational and occupational aspirations mothers and fathers have for their children was the last child-related parental attitude explored. Each parent was asked how far in school he expected his child to go and what occupation he expected him to pursue.

With respect to education, only 6 percent of the mothers and 8 percent of the fathers stated that the child's wishes should determine the amount of education he or she sought. A substantial majority of parents, 62 percent of mothers and 71 percent of fathers, said they wanted their children to go to college. The remaining 28 percent of mothers and 18 percent of fathers who responded to the

28. The Italian and Washington, D.C. data are reported in Pearlin and Kohn, "Social Class, Occupation and Parental Values," p. 470.

question wanted high school education for their children.

Educational aspirations for children in placement were far from the life experience of the parents themselves. Formal schooling beyond the high school level had been attained by only 7 percent of both mothers and fathers, and only another 21 percent of parents were high school graduates.

The parents as a group were more ready to allow their children to determine their occupational aspirations than their educational levels. One-quarter of the mothers and one-third of the fathers felt that the child should choose his occupation according to his own wishes. The remaining parents who responded to the question had a definite occupation or occupational category in mind for their children. Over one-third of the mothers and fathers wanted their children to be professionals. Doctor and lawyer were the most frequently chosen professions for boys, and nurse and teacher for girls. It may be of interest that, although almost all the parents in the study had had contact with social workers, this was a profession aspired to for children by only two of the mothers and two of the fathers in the sample. About one-quarter of the parents of both sexes mentioned specific occupations other than the professions for their children, such as secretary or mailman.

Parents of different ethnic and of different socioeconomic groups mentioned varying educational and occupational aspirations. Although there were some differences according to sex of the child, sex influenced aspirations less than did the ethnic or religious affiliations of the parents. Data on parent choices are shown in Table V.8.

Five out of ten Puerto Rican mothers, six out of ten black mothers and seven out of ten white mothers wanted

TABLE V.8

Selected Parental Educational and Occupational Expectations for Children, by Ethnic Group, Socioeconomic Level, and Sex of Child

	Percent of Mothers (N = 297)				Percent of Fathers (N = 137)			
	Education		Occupation		Education		Occupation	
	Child's wishes	College	Child's wishes	Professional	Child's wishes	College	Child's wishes	Professional
Ethnic group								
White	8	72	35	29	9	68	47	32
Black	3	63	26	40	2	91	22	33
Puerto Rican	7	52	14	46	13	54	32	38
Socioeconomic level								
High	9	65	30	33	12	70	37	32
Middle	4	71	23	47	5	77	25	34
Low	5	49	11	39	8	65	39	37
Sex of child								
Male	6	65	28	38	10	72	33	32
Female	6	58	21	41	6	70	34	38
Total	6	62	25	39	8	71	34	34

their children to go to college. Mothers and fathers in both Puerto Rican and white groups aspired to college for their children to about the same extent. The proportion of black fathers wanting their children to have a higher education, nine out of ten, was higher than for any other subgroup, and particularly higher than for black mothers.

Puerto Rican parents of both sexes were most likely to want their children to have a professional occupation, although they tended to be least likely to expect them to obtain the passport to a profession—a college education.

Relatively more white men and women were permissive in suggesting children make their own occupational choice. Relatively fewer Puerto Rican women and black men were permissive in this respect. Parents in the most deprived conditions were least likely to expect college for their children. Mothers at the high socioeconomic level were willing to allow their children to follow their own educational and occupational inclinations. Differences in expectations on the part of parents for boys and girls were minor. A further finding was that those parents who expressed expectation of college rather than high school, and professional rather than nonprofessional occupations for their children tended to have only slightly, and not significantly, lower scores on the alienation scale. Thus parental social alienation did not deter mothers and fathers from wishing for a status role for their own children in society.

PARENTAL AND MARITAL ROLE CONCEPTIONS

Since entry of children into foster care implies relinquishment of day to day parental responsibility, even if temporarily, it is of interest to know how mothers and fathers in such situations perceive the parental task obligations. Also relevant to further understanding of the study sample, in which only 11 percent of children were living with both natural parents just prior to placement, is knowledge of respondents' conceptions of marital roles. Data were sought in both areas. Parental role attitudes were assessed by means of a projective technique calling for spontaneous replies to several open-ended sentences designed to reveal the meaning children have for mothers and fathers. Marital role attitudes were evaluated from responses to items reflecting expectations and performances of wives and husbands on household and family related tasks. Findings on parental and marital role conceptions are presented separately in order to emphasize the differences between the mother-father and husband-wife roles, as perceived by respondents.

CONCEPTIONS OF PARENTHOOD. Four open-ended sentences touching on critical areas of parenthood were included in the interview instrument. Mothers and fathers were asked to complete the following sentences, with a brief and spontaneous response:

"For a mother a child is _____."
"For a father a child is _____."
"Taking care of a child is_____."
"How a child turns out depends on_____."

Analysis of the first two items provided an opportunity to report not only maternal and paternal responses for themselves, but their reactions as to the meaning of the child for the other parent.

The responses to the first two sentences, "For a mother a child is _____." and "For a father a child is _____." were classified into four discrete categories, only one of which reflected a clearly negative view of parenthood. This was expressed in the view of a child as a burden. A second category included parents who formulated their responses in terms of positive feelings for children; a third group referred to the emotional value of the child, primarily to themselves; and the fourth category of parents expressed their view of the child in a more concrete sense as an investment, again primarily for the parent. The distribution of parental responses is shown in Table V.9. Rationale for the categories used and relationships to other variables are discussed in interpretations of the findings.

Some parents completed the sentences with such phrases as (a child is) "a burden," "a nuisance," "a bother," "a worry," "a responsibility," "hard work." The number of parents responding in this vein was small, however; only 5 percent of the women and 9 percent of the men saw a child as burdensome for themselves. When these responses were related to reason for placement, women whose children had been placed because of child behavior or emotional disturbance were three times more likely than mothers with children placed for any other reason to see a child as a burden. A comparable view by men of the child as a burden was found among fathers whose children were placed because of the unwillingness or inability of the parent to assume care (almost all were illegitimate children). Men whose children were placed for this reason were almost three times as likely to see parenthood negatively as men with children placed for any other reason.

Both parents tended to overstate the extent of the other's

TABLE V.9

Parental Conceptions of Meaning of Children
for Themselves and for the Opposite-Sexed Parents

	Percent distribution			
	Mothers		*Fathers*	
	Meaning of child for themselves [a] (N = 297)	Meaning of child for fathers [b] (N = 297)	Meaning of child for themselves [b] (N = 137)	Meaning of child for mothers [a] (N = 137)
Burden to parent	5	17	9	10
Positive feeling	27	16	21	23
Value of child	28	22	22	17
Investment for parent	32	16	37	34
Other	6	8	10	12
Don't know or can't answer	2	21	1	4
Total	*100*	*100*	*100*	*100*

[a] Responses to "For a mother a child is ———."
[b] Responses to "For a father a child is ———."

negative feelings toward parenthood. Thus, although only 5 percent of the mothers said they regarded the child as a burden to themselves, 10 percent of the fathers saw a child as a burden to a mother. Conversely, whereas only 9 percent of the fathers regarded a child as a burden to themselves, 17 percent of the mothers saw a child as a burden to a father.

The great majority of parents completed the sentences "For a [mother, father] a child is————." with a favorable image. One group comprising 27 percent of mothers and 21 percent of fathers saw children as primarily generating positive feelings. They completed the sentence with such words as "warmth," "love," "joy," and "happiness." Caution is needed in interpreting these data, however, since parents of either sex whose children had entered placement because of neglect or abuse were more likely than other parents to express the view that a child is associated with a positive feeling.

Another group of mothers and fathers viewed children as valuable and important. These parents completed the sentences "For a [mother, father] a child is————." with such phrases as "God's gift," "a source of pride," "a blessing." Somewhat more women (28 percent) than men (22 percent) responded in this manner. Again, such responses are not necessarily a reflection of actual family relationships; six out of ten women with children placed because of abandonment or desertion completed the sentence "For a mother a child is————." in this vein, about twice the proportion of such responses for other placement categories.

A final category included parental responses in which children were seen as representing parental investment and reflecting a purpose in life. Phrases such as (a child is) "a reason to exist," "one's life," "a future," illustrate this category. About one-third of both mothers and fathers saw children as having such a meaning. Twice as many fathers felt children represented an investment for mothers as mothers felt was the case for fathers (34 percent as compared with 16 percent). Although there were no significant differences in the responses in the first three categories according to socioeconomic level of parents, there was a noteworthy difference with respect to a view of parenthood as an investment. A higher proportion of parents of low socioeconomic circumstances than those of high circumstances saw children as having this kind of meaning for them.

Finally, an interesting difference between mothers and fathers was seen in the capacity of each to empathize with the other. Mothers found it considerably more difficult to report perceptions of what children meant for the men than did fathers in reporting the meaning of children for mothers. Only 4 percent of the fathers said they could not complete the sentence, "For a mother a child is————." but 21 percent of mothers could not complete the comparable sentence, "For a father a child is————."

The abstract concept of what a child means to a parent is something quite different from the reality of how a parent feels about actually caring for a child. The open-ended sentence, "Taking care of a child is————." was included in the interview to ascertain whether the parents regarded child care to be a positive or negative experience. This is of interest considering the nature of the study sample, a group which for one or another reason has been temporarily relieved of child care. A reply was considered to be positive if the sentence was completed with such phrases as (child care is) "God's work," "wonderful," "easy," "pride." The response was considered to be negative for sentence completions such as (child care is) "headaches," "hard work," "difficult," "responsibility." A more realistic response which combined both types of replies, such as (child care is) "enjoyable and difficult" was noted as containing both negative and positive elements. As Table V.10 indicates, mothers were more likely to consider taking care of a child as a positive experience than were fathers.

One-half of the mothers but only one-third of the fathers noted pleasure or pride in child care. But half of the fathers, compared to fewer than two-fifths of the mothers, considered caring for a child to be irksome hard work. It is significant that parents of both sexes in the sample who were living in low socioeconomic circumstances were considerably more likely to view child care as a positive experience than were those in better circumstances. Fifty-seven percent of mothers from the low socioeconomic level as compared to 38 percent of high-level mothers and 51 percent of low-level as compared to 25 percent of high-level fathers perceived child care in its positive aspects. It should be noted that parents of the emotionally disturbed children, typically difficult to care for, tended to fall in the high socioeconomic group.

Replies to the last of the open-ended sentences, "How a child turns out depends on————." were intended to indi-

TABLE V.10

Parental Attitudes toward
Taking Care of a Child

	Percent distribution	
	Mother	Father
"Taking care of a	responses	responses
child is ————."	(N = 297)	(N = 137)
Positive experience	49	33
Both positive and negative	10	12
Negative experience	38	49
No answer or unrelated	3	6
Total	100	100

cate parental opinions on the critical factors determining a child's future. Mothers and fathers differed considerably in their responses, as shown in Table V.11.

Fathers tended to allocate responsibility for child outcome to both parents more often than did mothers. Of the latter, only 40 percent responded with "both parents," 27 percent said "the mother" and none at all said "the father." A much larger proportion of men, 62 percent, felt that how a child turns out depends on "both parents." Only 2 percent of fathers felt that how a child turns out depends on "the father." The women respondents thus more commonly emphasized the mother's exclusive role in determining children's future. Such an outcome was undoubtedly influenced by the nature of the sample, which included a high percentage of one-parent homes in which children and mothers comprised the household. Also of interest is the fact that

TABLE V.11

Parental Opinions on
Determinants of Children's Future

	Percent distribution	
	Mother	Father
"How a child turns	responses	responses
out depends on ———."	(N = 297)	(N = 137)
Both parents	40	62
The mother	27	6
The father	0	2
"How he is raised"	22	20
Other	9	9
No answer	2	1
Total	100	100

approximately one-fifth of both the men and the women emphasized the method of rearing rather than the parent per se. Those parents responded that how a child turns out depends on "how he is raised," or "on his upbringing," rather than on who raises him.

Replies to these open-ended sentences indicate that having children in foster care does not deter parents from reporting that children have a deep and positive meaning for them, at least in the abstract. For the great majority offspring were said to represent warmth, feeling, value, pride, or investment for the future. Parents of both sexes tended to overestimate negative feelings on the part of their opposite number toward parenthood, and a sizable number of women, in particular, were unable even to imagine the meaning of a child for a father.

In spite of the importance these parents assigned to their children, many of the same parents viewed child care as a substantially negative experience. Finally, mothers gave a more significant place in child rearing and outcome to their exclusive role, whereas fathers, more frequently than mothers, emphasized partnership of both parents as the determinant of child outcome.

CONCEPTIONS OF MARITAL ROLES. The complement of the parental role conception is the marital role conception in terms of both expectations and performances. The study instrument listed nine family related tasks, three traditionally performed by women (cleaning the house, washing the dishes, and caring for a sick child), three traditionally performed by men (repairing broken things, earning money, making major decisions), and three traditionally performed by both men and women (punishing the children, taking the children out, going to an agency for help).[29] These were read to all interviewed men and women. Each was asked two questions: who they thought "should do" the task in a two-parent family, and, in his or her own household just prior to the placement of the child, who "actually did do" the task. The intention was to differentiate expected behavior in marital roles from actual role performance. One hypothesis was that the single parent, who may be assumed to be handling all tasks alone, might respond uniquely and not conceptualize the traditional sex roles of men and women. This hypothesis was not supported by the collected data.

Marital role expectations and reported performances on specified tasks are shown in Table V.12. Expected marital role behaviors are presented for all mothers and fathers, whether living together or separately. Separate analyses indicated no notable differences in expectations for mothers or fathers in one-parent and two-parent households. With regard to actual performances, however, it is obvious that division of tasks was notably different for parents who were and were not living with spouses.

Data in Table V.12 indicate that the role expectations of the parent respondents generally follow traditional task allocations. Although both men and women affirmed women's primary role in the traditional female tasks, it is of interest that men, more commonly than women, indicated

29. The conceptualization of this area for the present study was based on the work of several investigators. A principal reference is P. G. Herbst, "The Measurement of Family Relationships," *Human Relations,* 5 (1952), pp. 3–35. The inclusion of this material in the present study was stimulated by the interest in changing perceptions of female and male roles, and in whether the study sample had moved along those lines.

they felt some such tasks should appropriately be shared activities. In particular men were more likely than women to see the tasks of caring for a sick child and cleaning the house as things that should be shared by both the mother and the father. Washing dishes, however, was designated as almost an exclusive female function by members of both sexes.

With regard to the traditional male tasks, the majority of both sexes tended to see two of the three, repairing broken things and earning money, as appropriately male activities. More women than men, however, indicated those activities should be shared by both spouses. The traditional (if questionable) presumed male prerogative of making major decisions was seen by approximately one-half the study parents of both sexes as an appropriately shared task, and by the other half as a male role.

The majority of study mothers and fathers saw the conventionally shared tasks as being appropriate to both parents. Where this was not the case, the man most frequently felt the task was one appropriate to his own sex rather than to the woman. Mothers' responses differed by task. Where they did not designate a task as appropriately shared, they were more likely to feel that they, rather than the father, should take children out; more likely to feel the father, rather than themselves, should punish the children; and equally likely to designate the father as to mention themselves as the appropriate person to go to an agency for help.

In general the findings indicate an acceptance of traditional role expectations by the study parents. For the sex-related categories, when either parent departed from the traditional orientation there was a tendency for both the

TABLE V.12

Marital Role Expectations of Mothers and Fathers and Role Performances by Household Composition

| | Percent expected to perform task[a] | | Percent who performed task[a] | | | |
| | | | Living together | | Living apart | |
Tasks	Mothers (N = 297)	Fathers (N = 137)	Mothers (N = 44)	Fathers (N = 54)	Mothers (N = 253)	Fathers (N = 83)
Traditionally female						
Clean the house						
Mother	84	62	70	38	83	—
Both parents	14	37	25	52	—	—
Father	—	—	—	8	—	22
Wash the dishes						
Mother	88	80	73	61	81	—
Both parents	9	16	11	33	—	—
Father	—	—	7	2	—	14
Care for a sick child						
Mother	75	48	75	41	78	—
Both parents	23	47	25	48	—	—
Father	2	4	—	9	—	14
Traditionally male						
Repair broken things						
Father	74	88	62	78	—	81
Both parents	19	10	16	18	—	—
Mother	4	—	16	4	51	—

Earn money						
Father	85	91	75	82	—	77
Both parents	14	9	18	12	—	—
Mother	—	—	5	—	32	—
Make big decisions						
Father	47	51	31	49	—	60
Both parents	46	44	46	40	—	—
Mother	6	3	19	7	60	—
Traditionally shared						
Punish the children						
Both parents	64	72	54	68	—	—
Mother	13	7	21	10	61	—
Father	19	16	9	15	—	27
Take children out						
Both parents	83	82	64	72	—	—
Mother	12	6	26	8	66	—
Father	5	12	5	11	—	23
Go to agency for help						
Both parents	64	58	56	50	—	—
Mother	17	12	32	18	70	—
Father	17	25	5	24	—	43

[a] Where totals do not equal 100 percent, a choice other than mother or father, such as grandparent or older sibling, was stated by the respondent.

men and the women to report that their own sex should at least share in the tasks typically allocated to the opposite sex.

How do the role expectations compare with reported task performances of mothers and fathers? Only a small proportion of the interviewed parents were living with legal or common-law spouses at the time of the interview. After the respondents were asked who should do each task if both parents were in the household it will be recalled that each parent was also asked who actually performed the task in his or her household just prior to the placement of the child.

Women living with men overwhelmingly reported that they were the ones who performed the traditional female tasks in the household. Except for decision-making (which was reported as being mainly a shared activity) most of these mothers indicated that their husbands performed the traditionally male tasks. Conventionally shared tasks were mainly noted as having actually been shared, but when this was not the case the mothers overwhelmingly reported themselves as undertaking them.

On the opposite side of the coin, men who were living with women had substantially the same view of performance. The main difference involved the traditionally acknowledged female tasks. Mothers speaking about their home activities overwhelmingly reported themselves as the exclusive performers of these female tasks; whereas the majority of fathers indicated that, in their homes, they shared with their wives or actually undertook themselves tasks involving house cleaning and caring for a sick child. A full third even reported sharing in dishwashing. Men stated that they themselves performed the traditionally male tasks. When men and women lived together, men were more likely to emphasize an exclusive role for themselves in decision-making, whereas women emphasized this as a shared task.

In those households where parents were not living with their spouses, it is apparent that women performed more of these tasks than did men. Where mothers were single parents, they themselves tended to perform not only the traditionally female tasks, but also the traditionally shared tasks and the traditionally male tasks, except for earning money. In one-third of the cases, however, mothers reported themselves as earning the living. Public assistance was the main source of support in most of the other cases, with alimony, child payments, and benefit payments such as social security supporting some fatherless households. The men living without spouses, on the other hand, reported the tasks they performed themselves to be earning money, repairing things, and going to agencies for help. Someone else in or outside of their households generally performed the remaining tasks for them.

The responses to this investigation of role expectations and performances indicate three findings of interest. First, the hypothesis that single parents would not conceptualize parental roles in the same way as those in two-parent households was not supported. There was little difference for parents living alone or with spouses in their conception of what mothers and fathers "should do." The second major finding was that, although generally supporting traditional roles as appropriate, mothers and particularly fathers leaned in the direction of approving more sharing of tasks, and more involvement of both parents with children. Finally, where parents lived apart mothers took on their own, the shared, and most so-called father tasks, whereas fathers' functions were limited to the traditional roles.

In summary, the investigation of parental attitudes has ranged widely over numerous areas, including social orientation, attitudes toward agencies, child rearing, parental expectations, and parental and marital role conceptions. Methods of acquiring attitude data have also been varied, including standardized scales, projective open-ended sentences, checklists, and forced choice items. Findings in these areas have been reported, and where investigations in other populations were available comparisons have been made. Conflicts and contradictions in attitudes abound, possibly as a reflection of the conflicts and contradictions that most parents face in the complicated tasks of parenting and child rearing. The factors most commonly associated with the attitudes of the study sample appeared to be socioeconomic status and reason for placement. The former was related to many of the more generalized attitudes, the latter to the more personalized ones, especially attitudes toward agencies.

The results on the social attitude scales indicated this was generally a group high in alienation as well as in calculativeness. With respect to agency attitudes, however, a large majority saw the agency as the facilitator of child care and were grateful for the services delivered. A small but important group saw the agency as a usurper of parental rights. For these parents the most relevant variables were Court jurisdiction of the case at entry into care; neglect and abuse as the main reason for placement; and parental feelings of anger on the day of placement.

Child-rearing attitudes tended to support findings of other studies which associated such attitudes with social class position. Preferred child traits, in particular, conformed to this pattern. An authoritarian posture in child rearing was expressed by most of the study group. Variations in the authoritarian pattern were related to ethnic and religious group membership. The negative or pessimistic evaluation of present-day society and life reflected in the high alienation scores of the majority of parents did not seem to carry over into their expectations for their children. Relatively large numbers sought opportunity for their children and expected them to achieve a college education and to enter a professional career.

In terms of role expectations and performances, acceptance of traditional views on marital tasks predominated, with some inclination to greater sharing by both sexes. The double burden of the single female parent was seen in comparing the role performance reports of mothers and fathers. The mother who was living in a household without the father undertook the full range of tasks—traditionally male, female, and shared—by herself, whereas the father living without the mother was not so burdened. A valid comparison of task performance, however, would have to include a wider spectrum of responsibilities of mothers and fathers, including whether or not they were employed outside the home and whether or not children were actually present in the home.

The responses of parents on the meaning of children to mothers and fathers are not easy to analyze. Taken at face value, they indicate strong attachment of parents to children, with the implied corollary that separation from their children is a traumatic experience for mothers and fathers.

On the other hand, it must be recognized that these positive feelings were in many cases expressed by parents who were known to be neglectful, in some cases abusive, often incompetent, and frequently inadequate in the parent role. One possible explanation is that for some parents socially acceptable rather than veridical responses were given. There is, of course, the possibility of such response tendencies in many interview situations. But the general consistency and quality of feelings expressed, as well as attitudinal responses, tend to belie these tendencies as more than partially contributory.

In the opening paragraph of this chapter the statement was made that attitudes are not necessarily predictive of behavior. The gap between the expressions of emotional investment in children and inadequate parenting behavior in many cases is not beyond credibility. The personal pressures and social problems leading to each child placement need to be comprehended as forces which often dissociate parental feelings for children from actual child-rearing behavior.

CHAPTER SIX

Parental Pairs

FEELINGS, attitudes, and perceptions of mothers and fathers of children in placement have been described, but as yet no comparisons have been made between the mothers and fathers of the same children. Such an approach requires the research problem to be conceptualized in a different way, because in this case the focus is on similarities and differences within each parental couple. By comparing reactions of the mother and father of the same child to the placement situation, as well as social attitudes, child-rearing approaches, and role preferences and performances, some conclusions may be reached on the nature of interaction, relationships, and problems within families.

The analysis of parent pairs is based on a subsample of the total study population, since it was not possible to interview all fathers in families where the mothers were seen, nor all mothers in families where the fathers were seen. Among the reasons one or another parent was not interviewed were, for example, institutionalization for mental or physical illness, extreme pathology, unknown whereabouts, or unknown identity. In 88 cases, however, both parents of the same child were interviewed separately by a study social worker, for a total of 176 research interviews. This subgroup of pairs constitutes the sample on which intra-family analyses were made.

RELATED LITERATURE

An approach to family interaction that involves studying parental pairs, such as that undertaken in the present study, brings into focus the inadequacy of the word "parent" when used as a collective noun. Parental research in the past has typically focused on one parent—almost always the mother —as respondent or data provider, not only for the couple but for the entire family. A review of the literature indicates that it is only in recent years that substantial efforts have been made by investigators to obtain responses from both partners.[1] Inadequate attention to the husband and father in the family constellation has been frequently noted in both child development studies and family research. Eron and his associates, in comparing maternal and paternal child-rearing practices, state that "A search of the literature between 1929 and 1956 revealed 160 publications dealing with mother-child relationships but only 11 with father-child relationships." [2] Later studies have remedied this defi-

1. The review of literature on marital and parental research included coverage of *Psychological Abstracts* and *Sociological Abstracts* from 1960–1970, as well as relevant books and monographs.
2. Leonard D. Eron, Thomas J. Banta, Leopold O. Walder, and Jerome H. Laulicht, "Comparison of Data Obtained from Mothers and Fathers on Childrearing Practices and their Relation to Child Aggression," *Child Development,* 32 (1961), 457–72.

cit to a certain extent, but information about fathers is too often obtained at second hand, via the mother. Nash claims that the neglect of research attention to the role and function of the father has distorted understanding of the dynamics of child development.[3] The dangers of this restricted approach have been summed up by Safilios-Rothschild, who questions whether research in the field relates to "family sociology" or to "wives' family sociology." She states, "There have only been a few family studies based on responses obtained from both husbands and wives. The majority of studies have assumed—without having tested this assumption with respect to all family variables—that the two sets of responses are quite similar and, consequently, have based their conclusions and generalizations solely on the responses of the wife." [4]

The difficulties and costliness of studying husbands and fathers, particularly in deprived areas and where there is serious family pathology, may well have discouraged many investigators. On the other hand, some of this matrifocal approach reflects former studies in which it was assumed that there would be no significant difference in responses from husbands or wives, and therefore both need not be studied.[5] Some of the presumed justification for utilizing a single family respondent probably rested on the earlier studies of mate selection, which emphasized the prevalent

3. John Nash, "The Father in Contemporary Culture and Current Psychological Literature," *Child Development,* 36, No. 1 (1965), 261–97.
4. Constantina Safilios-Rothschild, "Family Sociology or Wives' Family Sociology? A Cross-cultural Examination of Decision Making," *Journal of Marriage and the Family* (May 1969), p. 290.
5. For a summary of this literature see Ernest W. Burgess and Paul Wallin, *Engagement and Marriage* (New York, Lippincott, 1953), pp. 33–60.

tendency of men and women to chose marital partners with similar social characteristics, such as race, religion, age, class, ethnic origin, education, and area of residence.[6] Likeness in these broad social characteristics tends to define the field of potential partners.

Although the clinical field has recognized the importance of family experience and early relationships, major attention has been given to their impact on the individual patient. For many clinicians the patient's family was of interest only as a source of background material.[7] "It has only been recently," state the editors of a review of research in family interaction, ". . . that clinicians have begun to conceptualize the patient as one nexus in a family that is an interacting, stable system of roles and communications, with a transmitted culture of its own." [8] The need to study family life in terms of the give-and-take among members is supported by Safilios-Rothschild. In reporting on a cross-cultural study of decision-making and child-rearing, she suggests that it is "not possible to conceptualize the family

6. See the following as examples: August B. Hollingshead, "Cultural Factors in the Selection of Marriage Mates," in *Selected Studies in Marriage and the Family,* ed. Robert Winch and Robert McGinnis (New York, Holt & Co., 1953); E. W. Burgess and Paul Wallin, "Homogamy in Social Characteristics," *American Journal of Sociology,* 49 (1943), 109–24; J. H. S. Bossard, "Residential Propinquity as a Factor in Marriage Selection," *American Journal of Sociology,* 38 (1932), 219–24; R. J. R. Kennedy, "Single or Triple Melting-Pot? Intermarriage Trends in New Haven, 1870–1950," *American Journal of Sociology,* 63 (1952), 56–59.

7. For a notable example of a clinician who was concerned with total family treatment and research see N. W. Ackerman, *The Psychodynamics of Family Life* (New York, Basic Books, 1958).

8. William D. Winter and Antonio J. Ferreria, eds., *Research in Family Interaction* (Palo Alto, California, Science and Behavior Books, 1969), p. 2.

as consisting of the ever converging views, perceptions, beliefs, and values of both spouses." She proposes that studies of the family must be geared to a unit with interacting members including different opinions and perceptions. These may coincide to a varying degree in some areas and diverge in others.[9]

Two areas where both convergence and divergence can be expected in family interaction are role preferences and performances of husbands and wives and child-rearing attitudes and behavior. Hurvitz reports on role performances and role expectations for each other on the part of husbands and wives. He identifies differences between partners and develops an index of marital strain which reflects the gap between performance and mutual expectation on the part of husbands and wives. His research shows significant correlation between this index of strain and scores on individual tests of marital adjustment.[10]

In approaching the study of parental attitudes and behavior, Stolz conducted an interview study of 39 parent pairs and developed findings with regard to intrafamily similarities and differences in values, beliefs, influences, behavior, and communications. For the group studied, essentially white and middle-class, the fathers tended to stress basic values, whereas mothers stressed freedom from anxiety and obedience. On the whole, fathers tended to be more predictable in their behavior and more strongly guided by goals and beliefs in contrast to the mothers, who were more

9. Safilios-Rothschild, "Family Sociology or Wives' Family Sociology?" p. 295.
10. N. Hurvitz, "The Measurement of Marital Strain," *American Journal of Sociology*, 65 (1960), 610–15.

swayed by their feelings at the moment, by activities in the home, by communications sources, and by outside authorities.[11] It would be of great interest to study the possible influence of such differences in attitudes between marital partners on child behavior and adjustment. Friedman, in a study of parental attitudes and social behavior of children, found, for example, that the one area of parental agreement which correlated significantly with positive child behavior was mothers and fathers both expressing trust in their child.[12]

Data for the present study are primarily based on extended research interviews. Other research methods have also been employed, however, including review of case histories, attitude scales, checklists, and observation. It is nevertheless impossible to avoid some concern that the kind of findings secured relate to the method employed. This problem of relationship between method and findings has been explored by Rabkin, who has reported on studies in family research using a range of approaches and indicated the major methodological biases and their consequences.[13] Of particular relevance to the present study of parental pairs is Rabkin's conclusion that attitudinal approaches to the study of families will not reveal pathology, but that findings from such studies will, in fact, depend heavily on demographic variables. Thus obtained differences and agree-

11. Lois Meek Stolz, *Influences on Parent Behavior* (Stanford, Stanford University Press, 1967).

12. S. Thomas Friedman, "Relation of Parental Attitudes Toward Child Rearing and Patterns of Social Behavior in Middle Childhood," *Psychological Reports,* Vol. 24, No. 2 (1969), pp. 575–79.

13. Leslie Y. Rabkin, "The Patient's Family: Research Methods," in *Research in Family Interaction,* ed. Winter and Ferreria, pp. 5–23.

ments on attitudes will reflect social class, religion, and age, rather than normal or deviant behavior patterns.

PARENTAL PAIRS: SIMILARITIES AND DIFFERENCES

The present study afforded an opportunity to compare members of parental pairs from three different perspectives. First, mothers and fathers reported on why their children entered care and how they felt about it. These data reveal parental perceptions of the placement situation and the feelings of each parent about his or her own adequacy and responsibility in relation to it. The second set of data is concerned with the generalized social attitudes, feelings of alienation, and reactions toward social agencies of each parent. Finally, the data on perceptions of role preference and role performance as seen by husbands and wives illuminate some of the marital attitudes and reactions of respondents in relation to the partner. Thus the parental pair data indicate how each of the 176 respondents (88 men and 88 women) react: (1) as parents in terms of child placement; (2) as individuals in relation to social attitudes; and (3) as partners with respect to role preferences and performances.

The parental pair sample exhibits the range of social and demographic characteristics seen in the total study, although not in the same proportions because of problems of interviewing accessibility. Analysis of demographic characteristics by parent pairs indicates close correspondence between mother and father on almost all factors. Both parents were white in 30 percent of the paired cases, both parents were black in an additional 30 percent, and both were Puerto Rican in 33 percent of the cases. Thus 93 percent of the parent pairs were of the same ethnic group. In the remaining 7 percent, one parent was white, generally the mother, and one parent was black.

Religion as a factor presented more divergence than did ethnicity, but nonetheless among the pairs there were far more similarities than differences. Seventy-four percent of the mothers and fathers of the same child were of the same religion: 47 percent of the pairs were both Catholic; 17 percent were both Protestant; and 10 percent were both Jewish. In 16 percent of the cases, one parent was Protestant and the other Catholic. In 6 percent of the pairs, one parent was Jewish and the other was of another religion. The remaining 4 percent of the parent pairs were of various other religious combinations.

Both parents had had less than a complete high school education in 56 percent of the cases, and both had graduated from high school in an additional 11 percent. In the remaining cases the male members of the pairs were slightly better educated than the women. For 23 percent of the pairs the father was a high school graduate and the mother was not, whereas in 10 percent of the cases, the mother had graduated from high school and the father had not.

In terms of parental birthplace, both parents of a pair had been born in the same geographical section of the United States in 65 percent of the cases: 23 percent were both born in New York City; 11 percent were both born in the South; and in 31 percent of the cases, one parent was born in New York City and the other elsewhere, most often the South. Both parents were born outside the continental United States in the remaining cases.

In spite of the fact that the sample of pairs represented the most accessible families in terms of interviewing both mother and father, even for them family or household composition was complicated. Three-quarters of the parent pairs were married to each other, but just prior to the placement of their children, only slightly over half (53 percent) were living together. When the two factors of marriage and common residence were considered jointly, it was found that at the time just before the children entered foster care, 48 percent of the pairs were married to each other and living together; 5 percent were living together but not married to each other; 26 percent were married but not living together; and 21 percent were neither married to each other nor living together.

The fact that approximately half of the parent pairs were living together and half were living apart provides a critical variable for comparative analysis. It is of particular interest with regard to the reason for placement, as shown in Table VI.1.

When the 88 families are divided into those living together and those living apart, reason for placement is significantly differentiated in the child behavior category. Of the 21 families in the subsample with children placed because of the child's own emotional or behavior difficulties, 16 are families who are living together, and only 5 are families where parents live apart. Other categories do not differentiate significantly between the households where parents live together or apart.

PARENTAL PAIRS AND REACTIONS TO PLACEMENT. When parental responses to the question, "What was the main reason your child entered foster care?" were analyzed, it was

TABLE VI.1

Parent Pairs by Reason for Placement
and Status of Household[a]

| | Number of Pairs | | |
Reason	Total (N = 88)	Living together (N = 47)	Living apart (N = 41)
Mental illness	22	11	11
Child behavior	21	16	5
Neglect or abuse	11	6	5
Physical illness	12	7	5
Unwillingness or inability to continue care	7	2	5
Unwillingness or inability to assume care	5	1	4
Abandonment or desertion	5	1	4
Family dysfunction	5	3	2

[a] Because the size of the sample in each category is small, actual figures rather than percentages are given.

found that in only half of the families did parents agree with each other as to the main reason. In the other half they disagreed. Agreement between parents was high in cases where the placement reason was judged by respondents to be physical illness, and it was also high in child behavior cases. Agreement between parents was lowest in relation to neglect or abuse, abandonment or desertion, and family dysfunction.

In order to obtain some measure of the degree to which perceptions, feelings, and attitudes were held in common by the parents of the same children, a coefficient of commonality was computed. This coefficient is expressed as a percentage of the number of mothers and fathers, in matched pairs, who both expressed agreement on an item, in relation to the total number of mothers and the total number of fathers expressing agreement with the item. For any item the coefficient of commonality is obtained from the following formula:

$$\frac{2(\text{number of parent pairs where mother and father both agree})}{(\text{all mothers who agree}) + (\text{all fathers who agree})}$$

This coefficient is based on the same conception as the coefficient of similarity used in the cluster analysis technique, reported in Chapter 4. It should be noted that only agreements with an item, whether mutual or single, are included in the analysis. "No choice" items, where neither parent expressed agreement, are not included. Emphasis therefore is on commonality of affirmation or disagreement in choice. Mutual omissions are excluded.

Two illustrations will be given to demonstrate the formula. Of the 88 pairs, 16 mothers and 15 fathers said placement was due to mental illness of the child-caring person. In only 8 cases, however, did the mother and father of a matched pair both report that reason. The commonality of the item, therefore, is:

$$\frac{2(8 \text{ parent pairs})}{(16 \text{ mothers}) + (15 \text{ fathers})} = .52$$

A second illustration relates to physical illness, reported as the reason for placement by 10 mothers and 12 fathers, including 9 matched pairs. Here the commonality on the item is:

$$\frac{2(9 \text{ parent pairs})}{(10 \text{ mothers}) + (12 \text{ fathers})} = .82$$

The conclusion is that parental agreement, or commonality, is higher where physical illness is reported than mental illness.

Commonality coefficients for parent pairs by respondent reason for placement and household of residence are reported in Table VI. 2.

The difference in commonalities is substantial for certain placement categories. Thus, the commonality coefficient where child behavior was the respondent reason for placement was .79 for parents living together, but only .40 for

TABLE VI.2

Commonality Coefficients of Respondent Reason for Placement for Parent Pairs Living Together and Apart

Reason for placement	*Commonality coefficient*		
	Total (N = 88)	*Living together* (N = 47)	*Living apart* (N = 41)
Mental illness	.52	.63	.40
Child behavior	.68	.79	.40
Neglect or abuse	.15	.00	.25
Physical illness	.82	.80	.86
Unwillingness or inability to continue care	.47	.67	.36
Unwillingness or inability to assume care	.50	.50	.50
Abandonment or desertion	.25	.00	.40
Family dysfunction	.20	.22	.18
Other	.44	.00	.50
Total	*.50*	*.55*	*.45*

parents living apart. In cases of physical illness, however, commonality was high in both situations.

With regard to responses of both mothers and fathers about necessity for placement, approximately 68 percent felt that it had been "absolutely" or "very" necessary, with a higher percent of fathers (75 percent) than mothers (60 percent) expressing this reaction. When commonality with regard to the necessity of placement was examined, important differences were noted in terms of whether the parents lived together or apart. For all 88 parent pairs the coefficient of commonality on necessity of placement, reflecting agreement between mothers and fathers, was .59. Where parent pairs lived together, however, commonality on necessity of placement was .70, as compared to a coefficient of .49 where they lived apart. These data are of course affected by the higher proportion of child behavior cases where parents lived together.

Parent pairs corresponded closely to each other in expressing feelings experienced on placement of children. The only important difference, with borderline significance,[14] is in relation to the feeling of shame, more frequently expressed among the parent pairs by fathers than by mothers. Feelings expressed and coefficients of commonality are shown in Table VI.3.

For those feelings which were widely experienced, such as sadness and worry, commonality of feeling was understandably high, .88 and .76 respectively. Of interest are those categories where commonality was higher than the individual expression of a particular feeling. At the lower end, only 37 percent of mothers and 32 percent of fathers

14. $X^2 = 3.1$; $df = 1$; $P = .08$.

TABLE VI.3

Feelings Experienced on Day of Placement
and Commonality of Feelings for Parent Pairs
Living Together or Apart (N = 88)

| | Percent of mothers of pairs | Percent of fathers of pairs | Commonality coefficient | | |
| | | | Total | Living together | Living apart |
Feeling					
Sad	83	91	.88	.84	.92
Worried	75	69	.76	.78	.72
Nervous	54	54	.60	.59	.62
Empty	54	44	.53	.63	.41
Angry	44	56	.59	.55	.64
Bitter	40	45	.51	.50	.51
Thankful	48	54	.51	.59	.41
Relieved	47	44	.50	.50	.50
Guilty	37	32	.52	.53	.52
Ashamed	26	40	.38	.51	.17
Numb	15	16	.07	.07	.08
Paralyzed	15	14	.24	.18	.29

expressed the feeling of guilt. The commonality coefficient, however, was .52, indicating that about half the time when guilt was felt, it was likely to be expressed by both parents. This held whether parents were living together or apart, commonality being .53 and .52 for each, respectively. A different pattern was seen for the feeling of shame, expressed by 26 percent of mothers and 40 percent of fathers. Although parental pair commonality was .38, it was sharply differentiated by household status, with coefficients of .51 for parents living together and .17 for parents living apart. Other coefficients showing differences in relation to whether parents lived together or apart were those for feelings of emptiness and thankfulness, both felt in common to a greater extent when parents were together, and anger, felt in common to a greater extent when parents were apart.

Relatively high commonality was also found between parent pairs with respect to the most frequently mentioned referents for many of the feelings. Coefficients of commonality ranging from .50 to .89 were found for the following frequently mentioned referents: "self-child" for the feelings of sadness and emptiness; "other interpersonal" for the feelings of anger and bitterness; "self" for the feelings of shame and guilt; and "agency care" for the feeling of relief.

PARENTAL PERCEPTIONS OF MAIN REASON FOR PLACEMENT: CASE MATERIAL. Reduction of data to quantitative terms is useful to give a basis for generalization and comparison but does not give a picture of the specific nature of parental perceptions. For this purpose illustrations are useful, and the four case summaries given below will illustrate some of the agreements and disagreements of parents in regard to placement. In some cases parents may report different reasons why children enter care, whether living together or apart. In other cases, parents may report the same reason for care but provide the interviewers with entirely different pictures of the home situation. In the first two situations presented, parents are living together and in the second two, apart. In one instance of each they agree on reason for placement, and in the other they disagree. In one of the cases of agreement, parents have very different perceptions of the situation leading to placement.

300: Living together, agree on reason for placement

Mr. and Mrs. M. are a white Jewish couple. They have two boys, ages 11 and 8. Both parents were born in New York

City. Mr. M., age 34, is a college graduate. He is self-employed as a chiropractor on weekdays and supplements his income by driving a taxi cab on weekends. Mrs. M., age 33, is a high school graduate. She has done office work, but was not employed at the time of placement. This is an intact family.

Both Mr. and Mrs. M. gave as the reason for the placement of their older son the child's own emotional problems and their inability to give him the kind of professional help they felt he needed. Mrs. M. stated as the reason for placement, "his behavior at home and in the classroom. He could not conform in the classroom. . . . He does not know how to play with other children. . . . I was getting to be a nervous wreck. . . . I was pressured by the school to take him out. I was afraid to keep him all day. I just could not cope with him. Also, we had to think of his future. We hope that he will grow up to be able to take care of himself. We will not live forever."

When Mr. M. was interviewed several months later he stated as the reason, "the child's emotional disturbance—the way he behaved and our not really being able to secure the proper diagnosis. We tried everything. We hope that this school will be able to help him. . . . It was the only thing we could do if we look towards his future. We could not help him at home. I hope he will improve."

063: Living together, disagree on reason for placement

Mr. and Mrs. M. are a young black couple with four children, two boys and two girls, ranging in age from 6 years to 4 months. Both parents were born in the southern United States. Mr. M., age 27, has an 11th-grade education. He is employed as a truck driver and supports the family on his income. Mrs. M., age 23, has a 9th-grade education. She has never worked. The M. family was intact at the time of placement.

According to Mrs. M. the reason for the placement of her three oldest children was that she had taken her husband to court for non-support and the Judge ordered the children's placement. She stated, "My husband was drinking up his whole pay. He didn't give me any money. . . . I was taking him to

Court because he was not giving me enough money. We had to keep going back and forth to Court. The last time we went to Court the Judge said that the children would be placed, adding that it's up to me and my husband to learn how to get along better." The youngest baby, a 4-month-old girl, remained in her parent's care.

According to Mr. M., however, the main reason for placement was his wife's inability to care for the children adequately, coupled with the fact that she made "false charges of non-support" against him. He stated, "Their mother was incompetent to care for the children. I had to work every day. The children were not getting good care. The oldest child was missing days in school. . . . They needed help in learning the little things they should know like combing their hair. My wife could not do this as she was not correct upstairs."

016: Living apart, agree on reason for placement, disagree on situation

Mr. and Mrs. F. are a black couple with one child, a boy 15 months old. Mr. F., age 35, is a high school graduate. He is usually employed as a stock clerk, but at the time of placement he was serving a prison term. Mrs. M., age 31, has a 10th-grade education. She gives her occupation as seamstress, but she was not working at the time of placement and the family was being supported by public assistance. Both Mr. and Mrs. F. were born in the southern United States.

Mr. and Mrs. F. agree that the reason for the child's placement was his abandonment by Mrs. F. They disagree, however, about the situation surrounding the child's abandonment. Mrs. F. states that she left the child with a friend for a short period and her friend's husband placed the baby. Mr. F. states that his wife often left the child and that at the time of the placement she had abandoned him altogether.

Mrs. F. gave the following account of the events leading up to the child's placement: "I went out to cash a check. I left the baby with a lady. Her husband didn't think I was coming back. It was during the transit strike so I couldn't get right back. I came back later that night. . . . I depended on my friend. Her husband had no right to take the baby to the police precinct."

According to Mr. F., the reason for the child's placement was that: "His mother left him alone on many occasions. She would remain away from home for days at a time. Even when she was at home she neglected him and would not care for him. She eventually left the home altogether."

370: Living apart, disagree on reason for placement

Mr. and Mrs. M. are a Puerto Rican couple with five children, three girls and two boys, ranging in age from 8 to 3 years. Mr. and Mrs. M. are married, but they had been legally separated for one year prior to the date of placement. Mr. M., age 28, has a 4th-grade education. He is employed as a building superintendent. Mrs. M., age 25, has a 3rd-grade education. She speaks no English and has never worked. She and the children have been supported by regular contributions from Mr. M. and supplementary public assistance.

Mr. and Mrs. M. disagree on the reason for their children's placement. Mrs. M. states that she requested placement because of the children's behavior problems, while Mr. M. states that he requested the placement because Mrs. M. was unable to provide adequate care for the children.

According to Mrs. M., she only wanted two of her children to be placed, but she was tricked by her social worker and all five entered care. She stated, "M. [a 7-year-old girl] was becoming a behavior problem. She wasn't going to classes and would hang around with bad company. Also she would ask neighbors for money in my name. She really had me disturbed. Then I went to my social worker at the welfare center and asked him to put her in a school. Also R. [a 5-year-old boy] was behaving badly and was disobedient, so I asked that he be placed in a school."

When Mr. M. was interviewed, he stated, "What happened was that I actually took the children from her because she did not take care of them. She liked to go to dances. . . . There were always complaints against her by neighbors. . . . I took her to Court and then the welfare took the children. . . . The children were really badly taken care of and I had to do something about it."

These case examples, typical of others in the study, illustrate parental agreements and disagreements around placement. In child behavior cases, parents were more able to agree because the placement problem could be attributed to the disturbed youngster. Where questions of support or adequate child care occur, there are commonly strong areas of disagreement between mothers and fathers. Not infrequently, placement becomes a punitive action that one or another partner may take as an expression of marital disagreement. These cases serve as further evidence of the fact that child welfare problems are an intrinsic part of total family needs. Issues of mental illness, abandonment, incompetence to care, and financial support are played out against the background of intrafamily discord.

COMMONALITY IN ATTITUDINAL RESPONSES

The literature on family research has generally shown similarity of attitudes between marital pairs and has attributed much of this correspondence to demographic variables reflecting common backgrounds of the partners. This is borne out by the present study of attitudes of parent pairs with children in foster care. Close correspondence was found between demographic variables describing mothers and fathers of the same child, as well as between general social orientations of the parents. As discussed in Chapter 5, three social attitudes were studied: trust, alienation, and calcula-

TABLE VI.4

General Social Orientation and Commonality
of Agreement of Parent Pairs (N = 88)

General social orientation	Percent agreeing		Commonality coefficient
	Mothers	Fathers	
General trust attitude	*51*	*65*	*.69*
1. People will be honest with you as long as you are honest with them.	55	66	.73
2. Considering everything that is going on today, things look bright for the younger generation.	54	76	.68
3. It is easy to get along with people.	65	69	.68
4. Most people can be trusted.	38	42	.52
5. In spite of the fast pace of modern living, it is easy to have many close friends that you can really count on.	42	31	.44
General alienation attitude	*63*	*56*	*.67*
1. These days a person doesn't really know who he can count on.	73	73	.80
2. Most public officials are not really interested in the problems of the average man.	58	64	.65
3. In spite of what people say, the lot of the average man is getting worse, not better.	61	50	.65

| | Percent agreeing | | Commonality coefficient |
	Mothers	Fathers	
4. Nowadays, a person has to live pretty much for today and let tomorrow take care of itself.	48	52	.56
5. It's hardly fair to bring children into the world the way things look for the future.	49	30	.41
General calculativeness attitude	*85*	*95*	*.91*
1. A man should be allowed to make as much money as he can.	92	98	.95
2. In a society where almost everyone is out for himself, people soon come to distrust each other.	84	91	.87
3. Too many people in our society are just out for themselves and don't really care for anyone else.	80	78	.82
4. People will do almost anything if the reward is high enough.	75	76	.77
5. It is usually best to tell your superiors or bosses what they really want to hear.	48	64	.63

tiveness. The scale for each dimension was collapsed to a dichotomy for analytic purposes here. Respondents agreeing with not more than two items were treated as less characterized by the particular attitude, whereas those agreeing with more than two items were characterized as showing the attitude. Table VI.4 indicates percent agreement on each item and for each attitude for mothers and fathers as well as the commonality coefficient for each item and attitude.

Items reflecting an attitude of calculativeness received highest agreement from mothers and fathers. Commonality between parent pairs was also high, as would be expected, when agreement with each item was so pervasive.

Both alienation and trust were expressed by approximately the same percentages of men and women, with the overall difference that fathers scored higher than mothers on trust items, and mothers scored higher than fathers on alienation items. Commonality, however, was almost identical, .69 for trust and .67 for alienation. When these attitudes were felt, therefore, they tended to be felt in common. The trust item with the highest commonality, .73, was "People will be honest with you as long as you are honest with them." The alienation item with highest commonality, .80, was "These days a person doesn't really know who he can count on."

A significant discrepancy in maternal and paternal attitudes was found with regard to an optimistic-pessimistic view of the future of children. Children were referred to in one trust item and in one alienation item, and the responses to these showed the greatest discrepancy between the pairs of mothers and fathers. Thus 54 percent of mothers but 76 percent of fathers in the parent pairs agreed with the trust item, "Considering everything that is going on today, things look bright for the younger generation." [15] Consistently, 49 percent of mothers but only 30 percent of fathers agreed on the alienation item that, "It's hardly fair to bring children into the world the way things look for the future." [16] Whether the appropriate interpretation is that mothers tend to be more pessimistic, more realistic, or more burdened with child rearing, this finding indicates a general intrafamily difference.

PARENTAL RESPONSES TO AGENCIES. Attitudes of parent pairs to agencies as facilitators, usurpers, or surrogates were generally distributed in a similar fashion to those of the total study sample. The major finding was with regard to the commonality among parents who regarded agencies as usurpers. Although usurper attitudes were held by a small percentage of parents, when held they tended to reflect the common position of both parents.

Items comprising agency attitudes are reported in Table VI.5. Respondents could agree with from 0 to 3 items in each area. The response patterns were dichotomized for the purpose of examining commonalities between the parents. Because of the skewed distribution of responses, i.e., mainly positive for facilitator items and mainly negative for usurper and surrogate items, facilitator overall scores are lower and usurper and surrogate overall scores are higher than individual item scores.

Two-thirds of the fathers and three-quarters of the moth-

15. Difference reported is statistically significant: $X^2 = 8.1$; $df = 1$; $P \leqslant .01$.
16. Difference reported is statistically significant: $X^2 = 6.1$; $df = 1$; $P \leqslant .01$.

TABLE VI.5

Attitudes toward Agencies and Commonality of Agreement of Parent Pairs (N = 88)

Agency attitude	Percent agreeing		Commonality coefficient
	Mothers	Fathers	
General facilitator attitude	75	68	.76
1. It's a good thing there are institutions and foster mothers to do the job when a real mother is not able to take care of her child.	92	94	.94
2. If not for the agency helping with the children, many mothers would go to pieces in time of trouble.	91	91	.91
3. When a family can't manage a child, an agency can take over until he behaves better and is ready to come home.	87	80	.83
General usurper attitude	43	47	.63
1. If agencies would leave parents alone, they could manage their own children.	24	25	.60
2. Agencies act like parents have no rights at all—they think they own the children.	27	30	.45
3. There must be something in it for agencies, the way they break up families.	12	18	.38

Agency attitude	Percent agreeing		Commonality coefficient
	Mothers	Fathers	
General surrogate attitude	29	36	.38
1. Just because you give birth to a child doesn't mean you have all the responsibility of bring- ing it up—the state should take some re- sponsibility, too.	19	31	.36
2. Children are better off in institutions; they know better how to bring them up.	10	12	.00
3. When you come right down to it, the chil- dren belong to the government, so why shouldn't they take care of them?	8	3	.00

ers from the parent pairs saw the agencies as facilitators of child care, agreeing on all three attitude items reflecting that dimension. Agreement between both partners of a pair was high, the coefficient of commonality for the facilitator attitude being .76. Agreement on each of the three items making up the facilitator scale was also very high. The coefficients of commonality for the individual items were .83, .91, and .94, respectively.

Almost half of the fathers in the pairs and more than two-fifths of the mothers viewed the agencies as usurpers, agreeing with at least one item reflecting that attitude. Commonality for the scale as a whole was relatively high, .63. Thus, the statement, "If agencies would leave parents

TABLE VI.6

Child-rearing Attitudes and Commonality
of Attitudes of Parent Pairs (N = 88)

Child-rearing items	Authoritarian			Permissive		
	Percent mothers	Percent fathers	Commonality coefficient	Percent mothers	Percent fathers	Commonality coefficient
Talking back	86	82	.91	14	18	.50
Telling false stories	72	78	.76	28	22	.27
Hitting the mother	67	73	.75	33	27	.42
Picking up the baby	75	69	.68	25	31	.16
Hating the mother	42	42	.49	58	58	.63
Wetting	36	33	.45	64	66	.70
General child-rearing attitude	62	66	.73	38	34	.51

alone, they could manage their own children," was agreed with by only 24 percent of mothers and 25 percent of fathers, but matched pairs of parents had a commonality coefficient of .60 on this item.

Few of the parent pairs viewed the agency as a surrogate for child care. It is of interest, however, that there was a marked difference in response to the item, "Just because you give birth to a child doesn't mean you have all the responsibility of bringing it up—the state should take some responsibility, too." Agreement was expressed by only 19 percent of mothers but by 31 percent of fathers. Thus, mothers showed themselves to be less ready than fathers for state assumption of support for child care.

ATTITUDES CONCERNING CHILDREN. Among the attitudes explored with regard to children were approaches to child rearing and desirable child traits. The responses of matched pairs of mothers and fathers in these two areas present a picture of general parental accord.

Data on parental attitudes toward child rearing were focussed on the dimension of permissiveness-authoritarianism. Six sets of socially acceptable paired items were used, one reflecting a permissive attitude toward a specific activity and the other reflecting an authoritarian attitude. Data on responses of mothers and fathers and commonality of matched pairs are shown in Table VI.6.

Mothers and fathers in the overall sample, as well as in the parent pairs, tended to be authoritarian in their child-rearing attitudes. Sixty-six percent of the fathers in the pairs and 62 percent of the mothers chose the authoritarian rather than the permissive statement on four or more of the six sets of paired items, and could be characterized as holding a general authoritarian child-rearing attitude.

Permissive items were chosen less frequently than authoritarian ones, with two exceptions: reactions to the child hating his mother and wetting his pants. It is of interest that hating the mother was significantly more acceptable to both mothers and fathers than hitting her. Because permissive choices were infrequently made as compared to authoritarian choices, parents were considered to hold a permissive attitude if they agreed with three of the six permissive items and an authoritarian attitude if they made four authoritarian choices.

Pairs were more likely to hold an authoritarian perspective in common than a permissive perspective. The coefficient of commonality for a generalized authoritarian attitude was .73, whereas for a generalized permissive attitude it was .51. On the whole, however, the data show substantial agreement between parents in matched pairs on child-rearing attitudes.

DESIRABLE CHILD TRAITS. When traits chosen by mothers and fathers as desirable for a ten-year-old child are compared, there is substantial correspondence among selected items, as can be seen from Table VI.7.

The trait most often chosen by parent pairs as desirable was honest, with substantial numbers also selecting happy, neat and clean, and obedient. Commonality followed the general level of choice and tended to be relatively high for the frequently chosen items. The one item where it was much lower than the level of choice was in relation to "considerate," chosen as a desirable trait by 38 percent of moth-

TABLE VI.7

Desirable Child Traits Chosen by Parent Pairs
and Commonality of Choice (N = 88)

Desirable child trait	Percent choosing		Commonality coefficient
	Mothers	Fathers	
Honest	74	70	.76
Happy	52	53	.62
Neat and clean	48	50	.63
Obedient	47	47	.55
Considerate	38	38	.20
Self-controlled	33	28	.37
Dependable	18	22	.17

ers and 38 percent of fathers but chosen in common by only 20 percent of parent pairs.

ROLE PREFERENCES AND PERFORMANCES. Responses of mothers and fathers in matched pairs to who "should" and who "did" perform household and child-caring tasks were revealing of family differences. There was a large measure of agreement between parent pairs as to who should do the specified tasks, and generally both parents were traditional in their assignment of roles, as shown in Table VI.8. The majority of both parents felt that it was appropriate that mothers clean the house, wash the dishes, and care for a sick child. A majority also felt that it was appropriate that fathers repair broken things, earn the money, and make the big decisions. And most felt that both mothers and fathers should punish the children, take the children out, and go to an agency for help. Agreement between parent partners was high in this traditional assignment of tasks. The coefficient of commonality with a preference for mother on traditional female tasks ranged from .64 to .86. For fathers doing each of the male tasks, the coefficient of commonality ranged from .56 to .92. And for mothers and fathers both doing the traditionally shared tasks commonality ranged from .61 to .87.

Significant differences between mothers and fathers are noted for two traditional female tasks, with fathers declaring far more readiness to accept the concept of participation with the mothers in cleaning the house and caring for a sick child than mothers were prepared to assign them. Thus 41 percent of fathers but only 15 percent of mothers stated that both should clean the house. When it came to washing the dishes, however, both mothers and fathers assigned this task to the females.

Although high levels of agreement were generally noted on "who should" perform household and family tasks, such agreement was not so substantial when parents were asked "who did" actually carry on these activities. To obtain valid data for comparison of matched pairs on "who did," analysis was done only for the 47 parent pairs who were actually living together at the time of placement. Responses of these mothers and fathers, and commonality coefficients, are shown in Table VI.9.

There are two major findings from these data with regard to differences in performance as between mothers and fathers. The first is that, in the traditionally female tasks, fathers report that they participate in cleaning the house, in caring for sick children, and even in washing the dishes to a far greater extent than mothers report father participation. The second finding is that mothers report taking on sole responsibility for traditionally shared tasks to a far greater

TABLE VI.8

Marital Role Expectations and Commonality of Parent Pairs (N = 88)

Task	Percent expected to perform task[a]		Commonality coefficient
	Mothers	Fathers	
Traditionally female			
Should clean house			*.63*
Mother	81	59	.75
Both mother and father	15	41	.37
Should wash dishes			*.76*
Mother	86	80	.86
Both mother and father	10	16	.26
Should care for sick child			*.54*
Mother	75	50	.64
Both mother and father	24	48	.25
Traditionally male			
Should repair broken things			*.68*
Father	74	88	.80
Both father and mother	19	10	.23
Should earn the money			*.84*
Father	89	90	.92
Both father and mother	9	9	.25
Should make the big decisions			*.51*
Father	52	49	.56
Both father and mother	43	46	.51
Traditionally shared			
Should punish the children			*.64*
Both mother and father	75	77	.79
Mother	14	14	.13
Father	8	5	.11
Should take children out			*.76*
Both mother and father	85	85	.87
Mother	9	5	.17
Father	6	9	.15
Should go to an agency			*.45*
Both mother and father	65	58	.61
Mother	15	14	.08
Father	15	22	.25

[a] Where totals do not equal 100 a choice other than mother or father, such as grandparent or sibling, was made for "should do."

TABLE VI.9

Role Performances and Commonality of Parent Pairs
Living Together (N = 47)

Task	Percent who performed task [a]		Commonality coefficient
	Mothers	*Fathers*	
Traditionally female			
Did clean house			.53
Mother	72	36	.67
Both mother and father	17	53	.42
Did wash dishes			.55
Mother	70	57	.73
Both mother and father	15	32	.27
Did care for sick child			.49
Mother	66	47	.57
Both mother and father	30	53	.41
Traditionally male			
Did repair broken things			.57
Father	57	74	.73
Both father and mother	21	19	.32
Did earn the money			.79
Father	77	85	.87
Both father and mother	17	13	.57
Did make the big decisions			.60
Father	40	47	.73
Both father and mother	40	40	.58
Traditionally shared			
Did punish the children			.53
Both mother and father	57	74	.68
Mother	23	9	.27
Father	15	15	.29
Did take children out			.66
Both mother and father	66	79	.65
Mother	28	9	.35
Father	4	11	.29
Did go to an agency			.57
Both mother and father	45	60	.65
Mother	38	15	.40
Father	9	17	.67

[a] Where totals do not equal 100 a choice other than mother or father, such as grandparent or sibling, was made for "did do."

extent than fathers report mother performance. Fathers report more of these tasks to be actually shared.

The differences in reports of mothers and fathers in the same families with regard to tasks each performed may relate to variations in their perceptions of the nature and frequency of the task and the appropriate role for each partner. The father, who may wash the dishes once a week, may see himself as sharing in this task, although the mother may regard the participation as being too minimal to mention and see herself as carrying out this task fully. On the other hand, in a traditionally shared task such as taking the child out, the mother who has full-time responsibility for the child may report that she fully undertakes this task, whereas the father, with a full-time job, may consider that he has shared in it with a once-a-week outing.

FINDINGS ON PARENTAL PAIRS

The study of parental pairs calls attention to intrafamily agreements and disagreements, to commonality and differences between mothers and fathers, and to some aspects of family interaction. Data on the subsample of 88 families with children in care in which both parents were interviewed bear out some of the findings of previous studies noted in the review of literature on family research. There is generally close correspondence of mothers and fathers on demographic variables, as well as on social attitudes and attitudes toward agencies and child rearing. Within this framework of general agreement, certain specific differences are of interest. Fathers scored higher on trust items and mothers scored higher on alienation items, although commonality occurred in both instances in about two-thirds of the couples. In a comparable vein, fathers were more optimistic, mothers more pessimistic, with regard to the future of children. Although a minority of both parents regarded agencies as usurpers, when such an attitude was held it tended to be held in common by both mothers and fathers.

The majority of parents held authoritarian child-rearing attitudes, and commonality in parent pairs was higher on the authoritarian spectrum than when permissive choices were made. There was variation between parents on designation of desirable child traits, some held in common, others not.

Although the majority of both mothers and fathers tended to accept traditional role tasks, there were significant differences in male-female perceptions with regard to both preferences and performances in certain areas. In terms of who should perform certain tasks, fathers reported they should share in traditionally female tasks to a far greater extent than mothers said they should. When it came to actual performance, fathers stated they did share in tasks to a far greater extent than mothers gave them credit for. Mothers, on the other hand, reported they took on by themselves traditionally shared tasks to a far greater extent than fathers gave mothers credit for.

It is when the placement situation is studied as a focus of parent interaction that differences between mothers and fathers come to the fore. In only half of these families did both parents give the same reason for placement, commonality being highest when child behavior or physical illness was involved. On necessity of placement, commonality was higher where parents lived together than when they lived apart.

Both parents tended to report having experienced similar feelings on the day their children entered care, and feelings tended to correspond in most categories whether parents lived together or apart. One exception was shame, felt in common to a far greater extent when parents lived together. Guilt, however, was felt in common to the same extent whether families lived together or apart. It is in reference to actual case situations, where parents blamed each other for the placement and denied their own roles and responsibilities that the widest areas of disagreement can be seen.

Children do not typically enter foster care solely because of parental differences. In fact, many children enter care from one-parent or no-parent families. But where both parents are involved with the child, whether living together or apart, intrafamily differences can contribute to placement. Where desertion occurs in an intact family, for example, and is the stated reason for child placement, it is not always clear whether it is the child or the remaining husband or wife who is being deserted. Except for child behavior, where there can be attribution of causality to the offending youngster, or physical illness, where concrete medical diagnoses are given, other reasons for child placement may be interpreted as a kind of interference with family life. Inability to function when mental illness is involved, for example, may be interpreted by the marital partner as lack of adequate role fulfillment. This study of parental pairs who have experienced the crisis of child placement draws attention to both similarities and differences of mothers and fathers, most of whose intrafamily associations are played out against a background of severe deprivation, poverty, and pathology.

CHAPTER SEVEN

After Placement

FEELINGS of parents on the day their children entered foster care are only one aspect of study findings which relate to filial deprivation, or parental reactions to placement. Other areas explored in the research on filial deprivation include parental worries about children in care; changes in feelings from the day of placement to the time of the interview; visits to children; changes in housing, life styles, and situations of parents; and planning for and expectation of children's return home.

WORRIES OF THE PARENTS

Do parents worry about their children while they are in placement? Forty percent of interviewed mothers and fathers said they did not; 60 percent said they did. Approximately the same percentage of mothers as of fathers expressed such feelings. Of the parents who worry, the greatest number were afraid that their child might become sick or be hurt while in placement. Smaller numbers of parents were worried about their child's emotional adjustment, about whether or not they would actually get the child back, and about the possible loss of the child's love. Some parents expressed worry that agencies would not share with them information on how the child was progressing, and would conceal from parents agency plans for the child's future. Parental concerns about agency care did not necessarily reflect earlier acceptable child care practices at home; in fact parents in some cases projected as worries the very conditions associated with and contributing to placement. Thus, a neglecting mother might say she fears the child will be neglected, and an abusing mother might say she fears the child will be abused. Nonetheless, these worries were expressed by parents as part of the post-placement anxiety and were a component of the filial deprivation reaction.

Those parents who were worried that their child might get sick or hurt while in placement generally indicated three kinds of concern. First, they feared possible illness or accident. Second, they worried about whether the child would receive adequate medical attention. And third, they were concerned as to whether or not they would be informed by the agency of the child's condition. A typical comment by a parent in this connection was that of a father of a 12-year-old Jewish boy who entered care because of emotional problems:

I worry mainly if he gets sick. Will they let us know? Will he get the proper medical care?

Other parents expressed much the same concern. A Puerto Rican mother whose six children were placed after she left the home, said:

228

I always worry that they may get sick, and I will not be informed about it.

Parents expressed worry not only about physical accidents and illness, but about possible sexual abuse of their daughters. One South American mother of a 10-year-old girl who was placed after her mother's arrest said:

I worry about accidents, or her being raped or kidnapped.

An uncle of a 12-year-old Puerto Rican girl who was placed after her mother's death said:

I worry that something will happen to the girl with all those big boys around.

Finally, some of the mothers and fathers said they feared that the placement itself might be physically dangerous for the children. They reported their concerns to be based on actual experiences of their children while in care. A Puerto Rican father who describes his 4-year-old boy as "overactive, not right," and who placed him because his wife could not cope with him, stated:

I worry about his health. I hope he does not get hurt. Last week he got lost and they found him sleeping in some bush. They do not have enough help to watch the children.

A Puerto Rican relative talking about a 12-year-old girl placed so "she could receive good care" said:

One time we went to visit her and she was burned. Another time she was beaten up.

A father referring to his 7-year-old son who entered placement because he was unable to care for him after the mother's desertion stated:

I worry about his not getting into any accident. He fell off a flight of stairs two weeks ago. It is a miracle that he is alive.

In addition to physical problems, a number of parents were concerned about their children's emotional adjustment to placement. A black mother whose 6-year-old boy was placed because she could not provide adequate care for him said:

I don't like the way he is now. I can't put it into words. I just know him. I know there's something wrong. He's just like an old man.

An Eastern European father, who himself had experienced concentration camp confinement, said of his daughter, who was placed at the age of seven months following her mother's desertion:

She looks like there is no life in her.

Another mother, whose three children were placed when she entered a mental hospital, was concerned about her 2-year-old daughter's verbal regression, saying:

I worry about her inability to speak. She spoke before she went to placement.

An important area of worry for some mothers and fathers was the fear that they had lost their children forever, and that the children would not be returned to them. This worry was expressed primarily by parents whose children entered care either because of neglect or abuse or because of the unwillingness or inability on the part of the mother to assume the child's care (typically out-of-wedlock births). For the former category, legal procedures may be involved about which parents were anxious. In the latter case, the mothers feared that the fact that they did not assume care at birth would prejudice the authorities.

One unwed black mother, whose two-month-old baby was placed when she was hospitalized for tuberculosis, stated:

I am afraid that they [the foster parents] may become attached to him and I won't be able to get him back.

A 19-year-old Puerto Rican unmarried mother whose 4-month-old son was placed after she attempted suicide, was worried because:

I don't think I'm going to get him back. I only hope that if they don't give him to me that they put him in a foster home with rich people.

A number of parents expressed their greatest worry about placement to be the possibility of losing their child's love while he was away from them. The children in such cases were almost all very young, infants and toddlers under four years old. The mothers and fathers who worried about this made comments such as the following: "He may forget me." "I worry if they will remember me." "I'm afraid that she'll lose her love for me." "She doesn't love me no more." "My children may forget us and grow up to dislike us for failing to care for them."

A few mothers and fathers were concerned about what they felt was a tendency on the part of the foster care agencies to conceal from them important information about the child, and in general to ignore their parental rights. This often arose in connection with fear of not being notified if the children became ill or had an accident. One Puerto Rican mother with four children in placement, due to her abandonment of the home, said of her five-year-old son:

Sometimes I find him beaten up. They don't tell me how he is or how things like that happen."

A white Jewish mother whose nine-year-old boy was placed because of "his lack of understanding of his limits," reported:

I am not sure he is making any progress. There is so little communication with members of the staff. It is difficult to see them, and when we finally get the appointment, there is very little said.

Finally, there were a number of worries that parents mentioned related to the kind of setting in which the child was placed and the care he would receive. "I worry whether

they will put him in a foster home which I don't want,"
said one father. "I would appreciate it if they went into a
Catholic home," said another. "I'm afraid she won't be
trained as I would train her," said one mother. "I'm afraid
she will run away," said the mother of an emotionally disturbed girl. "The foster parents may get mad at her and call
her names—like bastard or something," said a 17-year-old
unwed mother. "I am concerned that they no longer speak
Spanish," said a Puerto Rican father.

When parents were asked about their feelings on the day
of placement, worry was reported by both mothers and fathers, as the next most commonly experienced feeling after
sadness.[1] When asked what they worried about, or the feeling-referent, the most frequent response for both mothers
and fathers was the child, followed by two related referents,
agency care and self-child. These three referent categories accounted for 86 percent of mothers who worried and
83 percent of fathers. The responses reported here on what
parents specifically worried about in relation to placement
therefore confirm the feeling-referent data. Fears for the
child about physical injury, illness, and accident predomi-
nate, followed by concern about emotional problems of
both children and parents and loss of parental rights.

CHANGES IN FEELINGS

To what extent were the feelings initially experienced by
parents sustained over the initial placement period? And if

1. See Tables IV.1, IV.2, and IV.3.

feelings changed, what was the direction and what were the reasons?

The study sample was limited to children in long-term care, i.e., at least three months, and the field interviews could not begin until the child had actually entered the sample. Thus, the earliest a parent theoretically could be seen was not sooner than three months after the beginning of foster care. With the problems of locating and actually visiting the home, the average elapsed time after placement was 5 months for the mother interviews and 12 months for the father interviews.[2] Feelings data reported for day of placement were thus retrospective and based on recall. Although this is a limitation on the recall data, the elapsed time had one advantage, in that it was possible to follow up on the reports of initial feelings. Respondents were asked whether they still felt as they said they did on day of placement, and, if not, how their feelings had changed.

Forty-six percent of the mothers and 58 percent of the fathers declared their feelings had not changed since the placement. As seen in Table VII.1 among those parents whose feelings had altered the majority felt better than they did the day of placement, while only a small proportion felt worse.

Parents whose feelings had changed for the better gave four major reasons for the change: (1) the child seemed to have benefited from the placement; (2) they had become resigned to the placement; (3) the child was now out of placement or expected out shortly; or (4) their own life situations

2. It will be recalled that, in addition to the initial field operation, in which 49 fathers were interviewed because the mother was not available as respondent, a supplementary father interview was conducted some months later, resulting in an additional 88 father interviews.

TABLE VII.1

Change in Parental Feelings from Day of Placement
to Time of Interview

	Percent distribution	
	Mothers	Fathers
Feeling change	(N = 297)	(N = 137)
No change in feelings	46	58
Change in feelings	52	40
Feels better than day of placement	38	34
Feels worse than day of placement	7	5
Feels both better and worse	3	1
Change, direction not ascertainable	4	—
Not ascertainable	2	2
Total	100	100

had improved. Parents whose feelings had changed for the worse gave two primary reasons: (1) the prolonged separation had increased their anxiety; or (2) the longer the child was away, the more guilt they felt.

Some parents who felt their children had benefited from placement were responding to notable improvement in child behavior. For example, one such father whose 9-year-old boy had been having trouble in school prior to placement, stated:

I feel a little better about it. He seems to be getting guidance there and maybe he will be better when he comes home.

And a mother whose 9-year-old son had had similar difficulties, said:

> I feel better because he's doing good. I see a big change in him. He's acting more serious and mature for his age.

Another kind of situation in which parents reported children as benefiting from placement involved preplacement problems associated with inadequate child care. One 23-year-old black mother whose hospitalization for jaundice and hepatitis had precipitated placement of her three infant children, said:

> My feelings have definitely changed now that I've seen how the children are being treated. I feel that the foster mother is just like I would be. She keeps the children clean, loves them, answers questions about them, and the children like her.

Another mother whose 5-year-old son was placed because of her hospitalization for tuberculosis stated:

> I would say my feelings have changed because I know my child is well and is treated very nicely.

A Puerto Rican father whose wife had abandoned the home and who placed his 4-month-old child because he could not provide proper care said:

> I feel better, now that I know he's all right. He gets good attention and care and I can see him.

A 25-year-old father who could not care for his three pre–school age children after their mother was hospitalized for mental illness said:

> My feelings have changed in that I see that the place is safe, that they have a lot of things to play with and they're well cared for.

A number of parents reported they felt better at the time of the interview than they did on the day of placement simply because they had become resigned to the situation. As one mother put it: "Time softens the worst pains." Other parents conveyed the same message in different words. "I got used to the idea of not having him with me," said one father. "I have learned to accept the fact that I can't have them now," stated one mother. "I have had time to adjust to the situation," said another.

The strongest expression of feeling changes for the better occurred among those parents whose children had already been discharged to them from placement or were expected to return home shortly. Mothers and fathers who felt better for that reason made statements such as the following. From a 25-year-old mother whose three children were placed when she was hospitalized for a gall bladder condition:

> I feel happier and more secure. The children are with me now.

A South American woman hospitalized for rheumatic fever said of the placement of her five children:

I feel relaxed—much better than before. The children are home.

A 16-year-old white girl who placed her newborn baby because she could not take care of him said:

He is home now. He is just wonderful. I am so glad that I changed my mind about putting him up for adoption.

Another mother whose three children were placed against her wishes by court order, stated:

I feel very much more satisfied. The Court and the agency are giving the children back to me.

And a black mother whose 2-year-old son was placed because a babysitter left him alone, exclaimed:

I am happy. He is back home!

Almost all the parents who reported their feelings had changed for the better explained the reason for the improvement in terms related to the child. A few mothers and fathers, however, said they felt better because of developments that had occurred in their own life situations. One such mother, a 16-year-old girl newly arrived from South America, noted:

I don't feel as powerless as before. I can think straight now. I think it is because I can work. I know I can do something for myself, and maybe for my child.

And a black father, whose wife had deserted the home leaving two small daughters, said:

> I have had time to get myself together. I'll probably marry again and make a home for my kids.

Only a small proportion of the parents reported feeling worse at the time of the interview than they did the day of placement. One of the reasons they gave for feeling worse was that they were anxious over what they considered to be a prolonged separation. A Puerto Rican mother, who placed four of her five children when she separated from her husband, stated:

> Every day I feel sadder. I need them more as time passes.

Another mother, hospitalized for mental illness when her baby was a month old, noted:

> I'm anxious to have her home. I have such pretty things for her. It hasn't been temporary. She is still there.

And a father, whose three oldest children entered placement because their mother was drinking and was unable to care for them, stated:

> I want them back. They have been gone long enough and should be returned. Children should be raised by their natural families.

Another reason given by the parents for feeling worse

was that the longer the child was away, the more guilty they felt. A white father who placed his 12-year-old daughter because she was "mentally defective" was typical of this group in saying:

> Now I feel more guilty. I know she wants to come home and I cannot even let myself think about it.

A mother whose 9-year-old son was also placed due to emotional disturbance said very much the same thing:

> I feel very guilty. Everytime I see him he asks to come home.

One mother, unable to care for her 6-year-old son because of drug addiction, said:

> It has gotten worse. My imagination is playing tricks on me. Sometimes I hear him crying—all sorts of things. He was very close to me.

Other reasons given by parents for feeling worse reflected their loss of parental role and rights. One mother, who placed her children to "be able to straighten out my life," said: "I feel very jealous toward the foster parents"; another, hospitalized for mental illness, said: "I cannot see them when I want to." "When I visit them they act like they don't know me," said a mother of two, and an 18-year-old mother commented, "I see other kids with their mothers and I feel bad." A Puerto Rican father said, "I am angry now. He was moved [to another agency] and they didn't tell me."

VISITS TO CHILDREN. The number of visits to children in placement cannot always be assumed to be a direct reflection of parental concern, since there may be interfering factors affecting their frequency. Agency policy, in some cases, may discourage or just not encourage parental visits; distance from the city may make some institutions relatively inaccessible because of the time and expense involved; finally, hospitalization or institutionalization may make visiting impossible for some parents. Given these limitations, however, and recognizing that the line between "didn't want to" and "couldn't" visit may be a thin one, the data still show a range of frequencies of visits which correlate in a meaningful way with other study variables.

Almost all the interviewed mothers and fathers had visited their child(ren) in placement at least once by the time of the interview. Only 11 percent of mothers and 10 per-

TABLE VII.2

Average Number of Visits Per Month
by Parents to Placed Children

	Percent distribution	
	Mothers	*Fathers*
Visits per month	(*N = 297*)	(*N = 137*)
Did not see child at all	11	10
Visited less than once	21	16
Visited once, less than twice	19	16
Visited twice, less than three times	14	14
Visited three, less than four times	9	4
Visited four times or more per month	15	6
Visited, number of times		
not ascertainable	11	34
Total	*100*	*100*

cent of fathers had not seen their children at all. Forty percent of mothers and 25 percent of fathers saw their placed children twice a month or more. Another 40 percent of mothers and about 33 percent of fathers visited their children on an average less than twice a month.

In Table VII.3 data on visiting patterns are shown in two ways: (1) the percent of parents who did not visit at all from time of placement to time of interview; and (2) for those who did visit, the average visits per month. Black parents saw their children less than half as frequently after placement as did white and Puerto Rican parents. Both black mothers and fathers were twice as likely not to have visited their children at all. When socioeconomic level is related to visiting patterns, both mothers and fathers in the lowest socioeconomic status were least likely to have visited at all. Of this group those who did visit tended to visit the least frequently.

As was the case in the analysis of other data in the study, reason for placement is a variable which is related to rate of visiting. For example, child behavior cases had the highest frequency of visiting, and the fewest non-visiting parents. The children placed for reasons of neglect and abuse, if visited, are seen almost three times as frequently by their mothers as by their fathers. The reverse is true for cases of family dysfunction, with fathers who visited seeing children three times as often as mothers.

Some contrasts in the data are revealed when parental figures on visits are related to age and sex of children, as shown in Table VII.4.

These data show that older children tend to be visited more frequently than younger ones and boys more frequently than girls. The figures are in part related to the rea-

TABLE VII.3

Parental Visiting Patterns to Children in Placement

	Visits after placement			
	Percent of parents who had not visited their children at all [a]		Median number of visits per month to children by parents	
	Mothers (N = 297)	Fathers (N = 137)	Mothers (N = 264)[b]	Fathers (N = 91)[b]
Ethnic group				
White	8	9	2.0	2.1
Black	16	16	0.9	0.7
Puerto Rican	9	7	2.3	1.5
Socioeconomic level				
High	7	11	1.8	1.3
Middle	10	5	2.0	1.7
Low	13	14	1.5	1.2
Reasons for placement				
Mental illness	9	3	1.7	1.6
Child behavior	2	3	2.6	1.8
Physical illness	12	0	1.9	1.5
Unwillingness to assume care	21	17	0.6	0.4
Unwillingness to continue care	12	20	1.7	1.2
Neglect, abuse	10	19	1.6	0.6
Abandonment, desertion	0	21	1.5	1.0
Family dysfunction	31	0	0.7	2.5
Total	*11*	*10*	*1.7*	*1.4*

[a] For mothers, during an average period of 5 months; for fathers, during an average period of 12 months.
[b] Does not include cases where number of visits was not ascertainable.

TABLE VII.4

Parental Visiting Patterns to Children in Placement
by Age and Sex of Children

	Median number of visits per month to children by parents	
	Mothers	Fathers
Age of child	(N = 264)[a]	(N = 91)[a]
All ages	1.7	1.4
Under 6 months	0.7	1.0
6 months to under 2 years	1.4	1.0
2 years to under 6 years	1.7	0.8
6 years or more	2.5	1.9
Sex of child		
Boy	2.0	1.7
Girl	1.8	1.1

[a] Does not include cases where number of visits was not ascertainable.

son for placement. Older boys comprised more of the child behavior cases, and this category was highest in visits. Nonetheless, the fact that visits by mothers increased with the age of the child is of interest.

PARENTS' VIEWS OF CHILDREN'S FEELINGS TOWARD THEM. Each of the interviewed parents was asked if he believed that his child's feelings toward him had changed since placement occurred. The majority of both mothers and fathers (57 percent and 66 percent, respectively) did not feel that their child's attitude toward them had changed in any way. Six percent of mothers and 7 percent of fathers thought there was increased closeness toward them on the part of their children. Seventeen percent of mothers and 10 percent of the fathers, however, thought their children felt more distant from them. Eleven percent of mothers and 10 percent of fathers said they did not know if their children's feelings toward them had changed, and data on the rest of the cases were not ascertainable.

FEELING CLUSTERS, CHANGES IN FEELINGS, AND VISITING PATTERNS. Relationships were explored between the feelings parents had when children entered care, the direction of feeling changes, parental perceptions of children's feelings toward them, and the visiting patterns of parents. Because of the complexities involved the data must be cautiously interpreted.

The identified feeling clusters at time of placement, as presented in Chapter 4, were examined in terms of reported changes in feelings after placement. There were some differences among the cluster groups in their reports of changes in feelings. For example, half of the mothers in Cluster Group A (with predominant feelings on the day of placement of relief and thankfulness) whose feelings had changed since the placement said those feelings had changed for the worse. On the other hand, every mother in Cluster Groups D and H who reported a change in their feelings noted that change had been for the better. Mothers in both these groups had reported a constellation of feelings including empty, worried, relieved, and thankful. Group D also felt ashamed, guilty, numb, and paralyzed; Group H also felt nervous. The number of cases contributing to this finding is so small it should be looked on only as suggestive. However, it may mean that mothers who expressed a more limited range of feelings, e.g., relief and thankfulness, tended later to have second, more anxious thoughts after placement. On the other hand, mothers who showed a wider range of concerns at the time of placement, as noted, apparently tended to feel better as time passed.

Among women who thought their child's feelings toward them had changed since placement, four cluster groups most frequently saw that change in terms of the child's becoming more distant toward them. This was true of Cluster Groups B, E, G, and H. The children in three of these four groups were predominantly young, under six years old. The mothers in three of these four groups tended to feel that placement itself was not at all necessary, and these four groups of mothers, who were most likely to feel their child had become more distant from them since placement, were also the ones who visited their children in placement most infrequently. The median number of visits per month ranged from 1.2 to 1.6 for mothers in these four clusters. The median number of visits per month for the other four cluster groups was much higher, ranging from 2.3 to 2.5.

Differences were also noted in the median number of visits to the children per month on the part of the fathers among the father cluster groups. Men in Cluster Group A visited their children least frequently (a median of 0.7 times a month). The children of these men were generally under two years at the time of placement and had been placed primarily because of the unwillingness or inability of the child-caring person to continue care. The men themselves were predominantly white and of higher socioeconomic level. They considered the placement as not having been necessary at all and reported feeling angry, bitter, and ashamed on the day the child entered care.

Men in father Cluster Group C visited their children

most frequently (a median of 2.3 times a month). Their children were usually six years old or more at the time they were placed, and they entered care either for reasons of the child's behavior problems or because of abandonment or desertion of the child-caring person. These men considered the placement to have been absolutely necessary, and felt relieved and thankful at the time it occurred.

A definite relationship was found between feeling changes and visits to the children while in care. Frequency of visiting the child in placement was associated with change for the better in parental feelings toward the placement. The median for mother visits was 1.7 times a month; but mothers whose feelings changed for the better saw their children 2.1 times a month, whereas mothers whose feelings changed for the worse visited only 1.4 times a month. The average for fathers was 1.4 a month; but those who felt better regarding placement visited twice a month, whereas those who felt worse visited only once a month.

In addition to the relationship between parental feeling change and frequency of visiting, a relationship was found between parent's perceptions of their children's attitudes toward them and the number of visits made to the children by the parents, as shown in Table VII.5.

Parents who perceived that their children felt closer to them since placement were the most frequent visitors. The visits of mothers and fathers who saw no change in their children's attitudes were next in frequency, and parents who perceived their children to be more distant than before placement visited the youngsters relatively infrequently. Finally, parents who did not know if their children's feelings toward them had changed visited the children least of all.

There are, of course, many factors which influence fre-

TABLE VII.5

Parental Visits to Children in Placement
and Perceptions of Children's Feeling Changes toward Parent

	Median number of visits per month to children by parents	
Perceived change in child's feelings toward parent	Mothers ($N = 264$)[a]	Fathers ($N = 91$)[a]
Child feels closer to parent	3.1	2.2
No change in child feelings	2.0	1.6
Child feels more distant from parent	1.6	1.0
Parent doesn't know if child's feelings changed	0.2	0.0
Total	1.7	1.4

[a] Does not include cases where number of visits was not ascertainable.

quency of parental visits, such as restrictions of agency policy, distance, expense, and parental incapacities, including illness and institutionalization. Yet there appears to be sufficient evidence to suggest that the visiting pattern is an important indicator of parental reaction to placement, or what has been called the filial deprivation response. Except for instances where parents saw unsatisfactory treatment of children in care, the case materials reveal that parental worries were generally alleviated when children were visited, particularly if they were in a satisfactory setting. Against these data must be placed the finding that black parents and parents of the lowest socioeconomic level tended to have the least frequent contact with their children in care. The extent to which lack of visits is voluntary or involuntary on the part of parents is, of course, a major and relevant question; but the fact remains that for some visits did not take place. Nevertheless, since positive parental feelings tended to be related to frequency of visiting, the vicious circle of those most deprived economically receiving the least satisfaction from the children was reinforced. The whole subject of parental visiting in relation to service opportunities and possible reestablishment of family life warrents further study.

CHANGES IN LIFE SITUATIONS OF MOTHERS AFTER PLACEMENT. The post-placement period allowed for a variety of changes for parents not only in attitudes and feelings but in their actual living situations. No longer responsible for the day-to-day care of their placed children, those women who were not hospitalized or institutionalized and who had no other children at home presumably had opportunity for greater personal mobility, even if their options were limited. Almost half of them changed their living quarters, a third went to work, and 10 percent reported a more active social life.

During the period between the placement and the interview, usually about five months, 45 percent of mothers who were seen had changed their housing. One-quarter of the mothers who moved did so less than a month after placement; another quarter moved from one to three months after their children entered care. The remaining mothers who moved did so three months or more after placement. Mothers of higher socioeconomic level were the least likely to change living quarters, most of the changes occurring for mothers in the middle socioeconomic group.

Changed living quarters did not necessarily mean improved housing conditions. Only one-quarter of mothers who moved went to a neighborhood which had a higher median family income and a lower juvenile delinquency rate than the one in which they had been living. One-sixth of those who moved changed to a neighborhood with worse rankings on these two criteria. The majority of women who moved changed to different living quarters within the same neighborhood.

Those mothers who had moved after placement were asked in the research interview if they had space in their new homes for their placed child to sleep when he returned. Almost half of the movers (or about one-quarter of all interviewed mothers) reported they did not have space in their new quarters to accommodate the child, should he return home. This is important data concerning the reaction of some mothers to filial deprivation. A sizable number of mothers, shortly after the placement occurred, had altered their living conditions, which could forestall the return home of their children.

Another clue to the extent to which mothers were actually planning for their children's return home involved the disposition of a child's possessions, such as his clothes and toys, after his entry into foster care. Somewhat more than half of the mothers (55 percent) left the child's things just as they were, ready for his return. Twenty-one percent of the women gave the child's toys and clothes to the foster care agency with which he was placed. Four percent of the mothers threw the child's belongings away, and 11 percent gave them away to relatives or friends. The child's effects were reported as destroyed by fire or lost by negligence or theft in an additional 9 percent of cases. Six percent of the mothers did not know what had been done with their child's things. In the remaining cases the children had no clothes or toys, having been placed from the hospital in which they were born.

Considering the multiplicity of problems faced by these mothers, it is of interest that approximately one-third of the mothers were able to go to work after their children entered care. The higher the socioeconomic level of the mother, the more likely she was to secure employment. Fifty-five percent of higher-status women, 31 percent of middle-status women, and 15 percent of low-status women worked after placement. As might be expected, the data show the most deprived women were least able to attain some measure of independence.

The majority of mothers reported their social life did not change after their children entered foster care. Only 11 percent of the women said their social life had improved since placement, whereas 12 percent indicated it had gotten worse. Substantially more women of higher socioeconomic level reported an improvement in their social life than middle- or low-status mothers. This may in part reflect the larger number of these women who went to work and were able to be away from the home.

Without comparative data, it cannot be concluded that mothers, after children went into care, behaved in a way different from mothers in families which had not had a placement experience. The evidence, however, shows substantial changes in these homes after children entered care. Half of the mothers moved, and half of those who moved did not have space in their new quarters to which children could return. One-third of the mothers went to work. Information on these post-placement occurrences and activities are relevant to the planning and implementation of agency services for families in preparation for return of children.

EXPECTATIONS REGARDING CHILD'S RETURN HOME. At the time of the family study interview, the children of 14 percent of the mothers seen had already been discharged from placement, and almost all these children were living at home with their mothers. Children who had originally been placed because of neglect or abuse, or because of the physical illness of the child-caring person, were most likely to be out of care by the time the family interview took place (typically five months after placement). Children who had entered care because of their own behavior problems were least likely to have been discharged from placement.

All the interviewed mothers whose children remained in placement were asked if they expected their children to be home within the next year. Fifty-six percent answered yes, 17 percent answered no, 23 percent said they did not know what would happen, and the expectations of 4 percent of the women were not obtained. Far larger proportions of mothers whose children had been placed because of neglect or abuse or because of abandonment or desertion expected their children to be home within a year than did mothers of children in other placement categories. The mechanism of denial on the part of these mothers appears to be strongly evident. Mothers whose children had entered foster care because of the child's behavior or because of the parent's unwillingness or inability to assume child care were least likely to expect their child's return within a year.

PARENTS' WISHES FOR THE FUTURE. The lives of most of the respondents in the family study have been severely limited and circumscribed in many ways. In order to secure some spontaneous expression from parents of their aspirations, desires, and goals, each parent was asked, "If you had three wishes what would they be?" Mothers and fathers, although interviewed separately, and typically living apart from each other, expressed wishes which were quite similar. The most frequently stated wish was "to have my child back," mentioned by 59 percent of mothers and 42 percent of fathers. Closely related to this was the expressed desire "to have a home with my family all living together," voiced by 46 percent of the mothers and 47 percent of the fathers. Other frequently noted wishes were for mental or physical health, money or financial security, having or finding a good spouse, getting a good job, mental or physical health for the child, and happiness. To a certain extent, there were differences between the male and female respondents. Mothers tended more frequently than fathers to wish for things related to the child. Fathers tended more frequently than mothers to wish for things related to finances.

The kinds of wishes mentioned and their frequency of occurrence can be seen in Table VII.6.

Given the opportunity to express any wish they could formulate, the great majority of parents expressed desires for a satisfying family life, financial security, and good health. Fame, travel, and "la dolce vita" were not within their aspirations. If judged by ordinary middle-class standards, such wishes would indicate that the parents were oriented to reality. Considering, however, the impoverishment, illness, and family breakdown that characterizes so many of these people, such parental wishes for the population studied do often reflect more fantasy than reality.

After children entered care most parents were worried about them, particularly about their health, possible accidents, loss of parental rights, or their children's love. The

TABLE VII.6

Parental Wishes

Wish	Percent mentioning as one of three wishes	
	Mothers (N = 297)	Fathers (N = 137)
To have child home or to be with child	59	42
To have a home with the family all living together	46	47
Mental or physical health for self	24	21
Money or financial security	22	34
To have, or to find, a good spouse	17	12
To get a job, to get a better job, or to keep job	11	22
Mental or physical health for child	11	16
Happiness for self	10	11
Education for child	8	7
Happiness for child	7	7
Child to be well behaved, a "good" child	6	5
Never to be separated from children again	6	4
Harmony in household	5	8
Education for self	4	4
To be free of responsibilities	4	—
Material things other than money for self	3	4
Material things other than money for child	3	1
Ability to remedy past mistakes	2	3
Improved relationship with spouse	2	1
Improved relationship with child	2	1
To live outside New York City	2	—
To have more children	2	—
To have help with child care	1	1
Long life	1	4
To escape from spouse	1	1
Not to have any more children	1	—
All children to be together	1	—
To have time and opportunity for pleasures	1	—
Spouse to reform or be rehabilitated	—	7
Health of spouse	—	4
To lead a normal life	—	2

fact that parents expressed worry about children's care in placement often had little relationship to the quality of their earlier child-caring behavior at home—in fact some of the worries seemed to be projections on the part of parents reflecting the inadequate parenting they themselves had provided. Nonetheless, the findings indicate expression of parental concerns to be a common reaction to filial deprivation.

A substantial percentage of parents reported that a few months after placement their feelings about it changed for the better. Such improvement in feelings was associated with more frequent visiting to children in care. The data show, however, that black parents and parents of the lowest socioeconomic groups visited children far less frequently than others, thus reinforcing a vicious circle of deprivation for their children.

Substantial mobility was seen in life situations of many of the mothers after placement. Almost half of the mothers moved, and one-third went to work. The evidence is fairly clear, however, that not all parents were anticipating an early return of their placed children. Just over half of those with children in care anticipated their return within the year. It is pertinent for practice consideration that half of those who moved reportedly did not have sleeping space for the placed child.

Parental wishes were in fairly traditional areas—family life, adequate money, good jobs, and health. Family circumstances and pathologies were such, however, as to make these goals often far out of reach. Neither the continued separation of the children from the home nor the return of the children to the home appeared to be the solution to the problems faced by these families.

CHAPTER EIGHT

Policy and Practice Issues
Related to Findings

KNOWLEDGE about the kinds of family situations which lead children to enter foster care has implications for both practice and policy. It would, of course, be an oversimplification to consider all the families of children in placement as constituting a homogeneous group. But with the exception of some families of emotionally disturbed children, there are many characteristics common to this parent population. These common areas include pervasive poverty, high incidence of minority group membership, frequent receipt of public assistance, one-parent families, and physical and mental illness.

It is apparent that the social service system as presently structured does not have the capability to provide basic preventive services to strengthen family life. A majority of the families in the study were known to social agencies before the placement crisis. Yet these agency resources did not prevent the movement of these children into foster care. The child welfare system is forced to operate like firemen arriving after the house has burned—fulfillment of its service task is hampered by the extent of damage done prior to agency intervention. Disadvantaged circumstances, extreme pathology, and inadequate parenting are common precursors of placement, thus handicapping the most sincere professional efforts to give such children a chance before they reach adulthood.

No panaceas can be offered here which promise a complete solution for the child-rearing dilemma. In any society there will always be some children in need of substitute parenting. But enlightened social policies designed to improve living conditions of the urban poor could effect significant reductions in the numbers of children entering care. Perhaps this can best be illustrated by taking a retrogressive view, and postulating what would happen to the foster care population in New York City if the Public Assistance Program, including Aid to Families of Dependent Children (AFDC) were abolished. The city would then be in the same position as countries in which no public welfare system exists, and where many children suffer grievously from destitution, homelessness, and starvation. If there were no AFDC program in New York City, the numbers of children for whom foster care would become essential would probably increase phenomenally. AFDC, criticized in some quarters as a program which encourages the break-up of poor families because of the presumed financial advantage of "no man in the house," should also be thought of as a program which keeps families together. AFDC keeps mothers and children together in their own household, and thus insures that children do not enter foster care solely because of poverty. AFDC thus reduces the actual number of children in foster care in relation to the potential number, were there no public support for these families. Moving from a backward to a forward look, other policies and programs need to be developed which would also serve as deterrents to the growing numbers in the foster care population.

This is not to say that the reduction of the foster care rolls is the primary goal of improved child welfare policies. It is an archaic conception to assume that the worst own home is better than the best foster home or institution. There are, in fact, numerous cases where placement in foster care may represent the optimal plan for a child, and possibly for his family. Such placement might be needed for a short or for a long term, depending on the case. Placement, when appropriate, may be interpreted as one kind of social service provided by an enlightened welfare system to marginal families.

The study of the natural families of foster children, however, leads to the conclusion that those families and children for whom foster care is the ideal treatment may be a small proportion of the total number of families who become involved in the placement system. Since separation of children and parents has repercussions which create new sets of problems for both, it would be generally desirable to avoid placement if at all possible, assuming that feasible alternatives can be developed.

Prevention, in the viewpoint of the authors of the present study, does not occur only at a single point in time but rather can be conceptualized as applicable along a continuum. All intervention services seek to prevent further deterioration of functioning. Thus, family services may prevent placement in the first place; working with the child's family while the child is in foster care may prevent long-term placement; services during aftercare and in follow-up situations may prevent reentry into foster care. All these services, in a sense, serve a preventive function not only on a temporal continuum but also with regard to a spectrum of family situations which extends from dependency and prolonged separation at one extreme to family reunion and independent functioning at the other.

The present study has revealed an obviously depressing picture of unmet needs and unfortunate family situations. Rather than merely summarizing data already presented in the various chapters, this concluding discussion will review the empirical findings in terms of their implications for policy and practice, with a view to stimulating development of more rational measures to meet children's needs. A certain risk is involved: data may be irrefutable, but policy implications of necessity must go beyond data to an overall view of the system, and therefore must involve choices based on social values held by the investigators. Thus the policy recommendations, although stemming from the findings, do involve a broader value-based view of the child welfare system.

FAMILY CHARACTERISTICS AND CIRCUMSTANCES. Data on family characteristics and circumstances provide important information on which to base recommendations for primary prevention. The study design was essentially a survey, with no control or comparative group of families in similar circumstances whose children did not enter foster care. Thus, any attempt at a definitive statement of why some children are and some are not placed, based on this study sample, would not be appropriate. But for those who did enter care, there were obvious circumstances which lay behind the placements.

Problems leading to placement appeared to be primarily attributable to the families and social circumstances and not to the children themselves, except for the emotionally disturbed group; and even for the latter questions may be raised about the influence of background factors. Although each case was assigned to a single placement category in the study for analytic purposes, the contribution of antecedent and intervening variables is recognized. Among these are factors such as the low income of most of the families, the poor housing, the single-parent households, and the disproportionate number of members of minority groups. These are among the socially handicapping conditions which put such families at risk.[1] When there is parental physical or mental illness, these families have few alternatives and the agency is often obliged to take over the child-caring role.

Primary prevention programs with regard to these contributory variables must perforce go far beyond the capabilities of the child welfare system, and depend upon broad national resources. Such programs would encompass an adequate family income maintenance plan, massive housing programs, increased employment opportunities, and a frontal attack on racism and discrimination in all areas, particularly education, housing, and employment. It may be that policy recommendations along these broad lines appear to be "belaboring the obvious" or to be too general when based on a study of families of children in

1. Shirley Jenkins, *Priorities in Social Services: A Guide for Philanthropic Funding, Volume I, Child Welfare in New York City* (New York, Praeger, 1971). For a discussion of the concept of the "socially handicapping condition," see Chapter Three, "Needs and Funding Priorities," pp. 38–65.

foster care. But belaboring the obvious is preferable to ignoring the obvious, especially when the "obvious" remains to be implemented.

Moving from primary to secondary levels of prevention, an analysis of the characteristics of study families provides clues for better ways to meet needs of clients. For example, the identification of groups "at risk" might make it possible to develop service programs that would provide alternatives to foster care. Such an approach has been suggested in the field of mental illness by Garmezy, who noted that the absence of proven knowledge regarding etiology of mental illness places a severe limitation on approaches to primary prevention. He suggests as an alternative, "vulnerability research" with the aim of identifying high risk groups.[2] This proposal is also applicable in the field of child welfare.

With approximately half of all families whose children enter foster care coming from public assistance rolls, a closer monitoring of the situations of AFDC families would be one kind of "vulnerability research" likely to have significant payoff in terms of early identification of problems. The need for placement rarely develops overnight. Physical and mental illness of the child-caring person, instability of housing and household circumstances, difficult child behavior and inadequate school performance, and the unavailabilty of a close extended family or relatives are all possible predictors of a future need for foster care. Periodic monitoring of these predictors could alert social agencies and allow them to intervene at an early stage. Back-up plans for

2. Norman Garmezy, "Vulnerability Research and the Issue of Primary Prevention," *American Journal of Orthopsychiatry,* XLI (January 1971), pp. 101–16.

taking care of children in the event of the incapacity of the child-caring person should be developed for AFDC families, based on the wishes of the mother and the potential resources of friends and relatives.

There are selected areas in which provisions for financial support of substitute caretakers should be liberalized, so that concerned persons who know the children could help in emergencies without adding to their own financial burdens. Steps in this direction have been taken for certain categories of relatives, but more can be done. There is no parity, for example, between the compensation paid to a foster mother who assumes the care of an unknown child and payments to a relative presently on welfare who takes a child, perhaps a niece or nephew, into her home and has the child added to her welfare budget. Care by relatives and friends tends to be less expensive than care by strangers, and if well done, should be far less traumatic for the child. The concept of "neighborhood parenting" could be encouraged, so that responsible families in the locale could exercise supervisory functions, if not actual care, of children in need. The development of resources in the community which could give actual substitute care in familiar surroundings without disrupting school attendance is one avenue which should be developed for marginal families at risk.

Supportive services to families in their own homes could both reduce entry of children into care and accelerate early discharge of placed children. An extensive homemaker program is probably the most specific service along these lines. Daytime or part-time help with child care and housekeeping could be particularly helpful to mothers who are able to stay at home and give children some supervision and security but who, because of physical incapacity or emotional difficulties, are not able to assume full responsibility. Homemakers can also keep families together where mothers leave the home, are hospitalized or institutionalized, but where there are working fathers in the house. One full-time homemaker can provide daytime care for three or four children in cases where the father works. This is a plan which costs a fraction of that for foster care in a multiple placement, and if well done meets children's needs by maintaining home and family ties.

REASONS FOR PLACEMENT. The analysis of placement reasons in Chapter 3 suggests a number of policy recommendations for dealing with foster care needs. These recommendations are not startling, new, or original to this study; they are based on needs which have been apparent for a long time. But since these needs largely remain unmet, the proposals must be reiterated.

There are many kinds of service needs which are relevant to child placement, but which are not necessarily lodged in the child welfare field, although they are specific and can be identified. For example, many of the mentally ill mothers, who comprise an important part of the study sample, might have benefited from out-patient treatment at community mental health centers, and even might have been kept from institutional placement if they had had access to supportive services such as day care centers and homemakers. Expansion of school social work for early case finding, special day schools for children with emotional problems, and family treatment services which reach out to the community would help keep many disturbed children at home. Effective and non-discriminatory administration of the new laws and programs for abortion should make for a sharp reduction in numbers of abandoned infants, as would a broadly based family planning program. This is not an exhaustive listing by any means, but an indication of some of the social and health services which could help keep children with their own families.

There will always be some children, however, who cannot be retained at home or in the community, and others who should not stay at home. The latter refers primarily to the neglect and abuse group. There is no easy solution to the problem of abusive parents. Placement should be for child protection, not parental punishment, and in some cases long-term care must be planned. The premature return of a child to a home which continues to be abusive does no credit to the foster care system. There is need for reevaluation of the approach to abusive parents, with follow-up care and supervision of the home being an integral part of the social work process. A recent national study on abusive parents suggests that the violence in abuse cases reflects widespread acceptance of corporal punishment in child rearing, as well as the subservient position allocated to children in our society.[3] This hypothesis supports the implication already stated—that problems of child welfare need solutions beyond the capability of the established child welfare service system.

There has been substantial discussion in this study of the individual reasons for placement of children. The data suggest, however, that a further line of analysis would be to look at selected groupings of reasons and see what ad-

3. David Gil, *Violence Against Children: Physical Child Abuse in the United States* (Cambridge, Harvard University Press, 1970).

ditional insights can be obtained. For example, "socially acceptable" reasons for placement, e.g., mental or physical illness of the mother or emotional problems of the children, can be compared with a grouping which may be called "socially disapproved" reasons for placement, e.g., abuse, neglect, abandonment, and severe family dysfunction. Data on the experiences of these natural families with foster care will be analyzed according to this typology in a follow-up study to the present research.

FEELINGS OF PARENTS. A major aspect of this research is the attention given to the feelings of parents when children are placed and to their reactions to the filial deprivation they have experienced. The findings, which are presented in detail in Chapter 4, have important practice implications.

The parental feelings in response to placement of their children can be described as running the gamut from sadness to relief, from anger to thankfulness, from shame to worry. But the main finding was not the accounting of a variety of feelings, but rather the patterns or identifiable clusters of feelings held in common by different groups of mothers and fathers. These clusters were found to be associated with socioeconomic level, case jurisdiction, ethnic group, and reason for placement.

Almost all parents experienced some emotional reaction when children entered care. Sadness is the overriding feeling reported. But relief and thankfulness were also noted, as were guilt and shame, and these feelings tend to be situation oriented. Anger at placement is a significant indicator of certain placement problems. An important question for practice is the extent to which agencies and casework staff who "work with families" try to understand and work constructively with parental feelings on placement.

Factor analysis of the correlation matrices of feelings and their referents in the study led to the identification of six major factors: interpersonal hostility, separation anxiety with sadness, self-denigration, agency hostility, concerned gratitude, and self-involvement. The findings on referents of the feelings point to the importance of self—that is, the mothers' and fathers' concern with their own needs and problems. Furthermore, although some hostility was directed toward the agencies, the bulk of angry feelings were interpersonal, frequently directed against the other parent of the child and sometimes against the respondent's own parent.

Parental reactions to placement which are relevant for practice can be summarized in three general areas. First, workers need to recognize that parental feelings to separation from their children are varied and complex. They are not unidimensional, nor are they irrational or totally scattered. For many parents such feelings fall into definable clusters. In the second place, these clusters are often related to reasons for placement as well as demographic and socioeconomic characteristics and attitudinal patterns. Thus, a study of parental feelings may provide a kind of mapping to help workers develop an individualized approach to different situations. The third implication of these data for practice relates primarily to the material on referents. Self and interpersonal referents rather than child referents, dominate parental feelings about many aspects of placement. An approach to parents which focuses only on child needs and ignores parental concerns with their own problems is not likely to be effective.

ATTITUDES AND SERVICES. Parents with children in care respond to general attitudinal questions in a predictable way; the responses are differentiated along socioeconomic and ethnic lines. Most parents tend to have an alienated and calculating orientation; they express authoritarian child rearing attitudes; their choices of preferred child traits are the same as those of other low-income groups; and they generally accept traditional marital roles in family life.

When attitudes which relate specifically to the placement situation rather than to generalized social themes are analyzed, a somewhat different picture emerges. In spite of strong apparent alienation from society, most parents regarded agencies as facilitators of child care and helpful to families in times of crisis. A vocal minority, however, saw agencies as usurpers of their parental rights. Others perceived agencies as parent surrogates. Each of these three attitudinal valuations has a different but relevant implication for practice. Knowing how parents perceive agencies can help workers in their efforts to facilitate discharge.

Another finding on differences between generalized and individualized attitudes is with regard to expectations for children. In response to the alienation items, a substantial number of mothers and fathers agreed that this is a difficult time for the younger generation, and that it is hardly fair to bring children into the world as it is today. But when asked about their anticipations and wishes for the future of their own children, a large majority wanted college for their youngsters and a chance to enter the professions, under the assumption that these would involve social and economic rewards.

The study of parental pairs gave evidence on areas of agreement and disagreement between mothers and fathers, and also on differences between generalized and specific attitudes and feelings. Commonality between parents was high, whether they were living together or apart, on demographic variables, generalized social attitudes, agency attitudes, and child rearing. Where there were significant differences, these related to marital role expectations and performances and perceptions on the part of parents of their own relationship to the placement situations. In only half of the families, for example, did mothers and fathers state the same reason for placement; and when there was agreement, it occurred primarily in cases of child behavior or physical illness of the child-caring person. This finding also has practice implications, in that some common understanding between parents on why the child entered care is an obvious area of concern for the social worker.

The evidence that agreement on broad issues does not necessarily mean agreement on specific questions has some general implications. Generalized attitudes tend to relate to the socioeconomic position of respondents, but specific attitudes relate to their individualized needs and experiences. These usually co-relate, but they may be at variance. Thus when there are issues in which parents have a particular stake, they may react differently than they would if abstract, generalized views were sought.

A further implication of this difference between general and specific perception is that, although positive attitudes toward a particular agency may be developed because of specific individual experiences, these are not likely to affect the generalized social attitudes of the poor and near-poor. The related research literature shows the close correspondence between social attitudes of the study sample and those of comparable families where placement of children is not involved, indicating how pervasive certain attitude sets can be. Thus a corollary to the postulate that casework services alone will not change poverty is that a specific attitude toward agencies, based on an individual service, is often not predictive of basic social attitudes. The latter are generally related to poverty, class, and ethnic group and correspond closely for both placement and non-placement groups.

DURING AND AFTER PLACEMENT. The concept of filial deprivation, which the present research has only begun to examine, has important implications for policy as well as practice. Feelings related to placement, as already noted, represent important data for working with parents during placement and at discharge. There are also other postplacement findings in addition to feelings which are related to filial deprivation. The extent of parental worry, and the things parents worry about when children are in care, comprise important information for child welfare agencies. Parents frequently expressed concern that they would not be informed if children were ill or injured, that they would lose touch with children and lose their love, and that parental rights would be lost.

For about half of all parents, feelings tended to change after some months in placement, and most of the parents whose feelings changed reported reduction in anxiety. This may be a possible gain for parents, but it is also a warning to agencies that the sense of loss may diminish over time. Long separations may become unnecessarily prolonged. Less urgency for discharge was expressed by parents the longer the child was in care. The importance of acting quickly to expedite reunion is thus emphasized.

Visits to children while in care need to be analyzed in terms of parental initiative and mobility, as well as agency policies which may discourage rather than encourage parent-child contact. The fact that the youngest children, the black children, and the poorest children were visited least frequently speaks for the irrationality of the system. There is need to examine visiting policies in relation to maintenance of family communication and interaction.

AGENDA FOR SOCIAL POLICY. The family research program involves a longitudinal study which will ultimately span five years after the entry of children into care. The present volume presents findings based on interviews with natural parents shortly after children entered placement. Thus the data constitute baseline information about the circumstances, characteristics, feelings, and attitudes of the mothers and fathers soon after the placement experience. Two follow-up sets of interviews, one at two and one-half and the other at five years after placement, are designed to collect further data on experiences of families while children are still in care or subsequent to discharge.[4] Three major items on the social policy agenda are generated by the study findings. The first suggests child advocacy; the second is concerned with parental rights; and the third stresses the need for integration of social services to effect both primary and secondary prevention in the social welfare field.

Although this study has focused on the parents of children in placement, especially the mothers, the background data on circumstances and characteristics of the families document how difficult are the life situations of children

4. The initial interview was in 1966; the second was completed in 1968; the third in 1971. These all deal with family data.

who enter placement. Recommendations and even provisions for supportive services may be on the books, but for the child who is abandoned or deserted, neglected or abused, or cared for by parents who are physically or mentally ill, there is need for responsible social intervention and for public or private assumption of the role of child advocate to protect and nurture the minor citizen. This formulation does not postulate child advocacy as assuming an adversary position in relation to family needs. Indeed, helping the family may well be the best way to help the child. The special "watchdog" role of child protector is still necessary in the case of the abused child, but the advocacy principal is far broader, referring to support for all provinces designed to improve the status of children. On an individual basis, by and large, for most children it is a reasonable assumption that their best advocates are their own parents. But when the parents as a group are not effective in the political arena, organized social welfare can play an important role.

Parental rights also emerge as a matter of increasing concern. For any poverty group, there is a built-in problem of equity in access to available resources. Children can be removed from and returned to parental care for a range of reasons—some appropriate, some not—and these reasons may reflect arbitrary, discriminatory, or capricious decisions. One part of the problem in New York City, for example, is that for the large Spanish-speaking population decisions on child care may be based on inadequate comprehension of language or life style.

A further complication with regard to parental rights is the uncertainty of the agency care offered the child. Where is the accountability? Who is the consumer of child care services? Does the parent, for example, when the child enters care, assume the role of "guilty party," to be investigated and rehabilitated, or does he assume the role of citizen with the right to information on how the child care agency functions and about the quality of care delivered? Can he exercise freedom of choice—can he say he wants his child to receive this and not that kind of care? Can he be involved in evaluating agency personnel and actions? These questions may seem out of order when in fact the real issue is whether the parent has any parental rights at all and, if he has rights, whether he knows them. In an era when soldiers assert their civil rights, clients their welfare rights, and students their academic rights, mothers and fathers of children in care can be expected to assert their parental rights. The social welfare field will have to prepare itself for a new dialogue with such parents.

Finally, the most pervasive implication of the study findings relates to the need for a unified social welfare system, the only way to bring rationality into the present chaos. The focus of social work should not be on the multiproblem family. This is a distortion of the need. The focus has to be on the multiproblem society, where the interrelationships are such that poverty, mental illness, unemployment, racism, poor housing, and other ills too well known to mention feed and exacerbate each other. The problems of foster care are only symptomatic of broader issues, and child welfare services are only an interim, although necessary, palliative. An integrated welfare system must operate on a micro as well as macro basis. It should mean out-patient services, day care, and homemaker help for mothers with emotional problems who can be maintained in the community; it should mean a broadly based educational system with a network of day schools, including neighborhood residential centers for children who have special problems. It should mean family planning and an effective abortion system, as well as housing for unwed mothers and their babies and nurseries and job training centers. The list is endless. An integrated, effective social welfare system should, in fact, mean the development of programs not yet conceived because we have been locked into a system of crisis child care.

Construction of the Index of Socioeconomic Circumstances

THE INDEX of socioeconomic circumstances was designed to differentiate within a relatively homogeneous sample, and the variables incorporated in the index were selected to reflect the characteristics relevant for these families. The majority of the study sample experienced one or more situations found in poverty populations, i.e., female-headed households, deteriorated housing, support from public assistance, and lack of an adult working member. Variables utilized in conventional indexes, such as "occupation" and "amount of income," were therefore inappropriate for use with this group.

A socioeconomic index incorporating five variables appropriate to the sample was developed. They are: (1) main source of support; (2) education; (3) income rank of neighborhood; (4) juvenile delinquency rank of neighborhood; and (5) number of negative housing conditions. A detailed account of the content of the variables, and of the procedures for weighting each and constructing the index, follows.

VARIABLE 1: MAIN SOURCE OF SUPPORT. Households in the study were supported primarily by either public assistance or salaries, with a small group having other main sources such as benefit payments, alimony payments, or help from friends or relatives. A few households had no known source of support, or the main source of support was not ascertainable. In scaling this particular variable, differentiation was made within the two large modal groups. Those households with salaries were divided into three groups, according to the total amount of income coming into the home. The public assistance households were divided into three groups according to length of time such aid had been received.

The final support scale contained seven intervals. Those households which had salaries as the main source of support and had the highest total amount of income ($100 per week or more) were given first or highest ranking, followed by the next two categories of income level. Those households which had public assistance as the main source of support and had received such assistance for the longest period of time (six years or more) were given seventh or lowest ranking, and the next two categories above them reflected shorter periods of time on welfare. The middle rank of four in the seven-interval scale was given to those households where the main source of support was benefit or alimony payments, or help from friends or relatives. For the few cases where the main source of support was not ascertainable, the household was also given the middle scale rank of four.

Since such an attempt at unidimensional scaling essentially involves a series of value judgments on inclusions, exclusions, and rankings which are not culture-free, it is relevant to state some of the assumptions underlying the choice and formulation of variables. One basic assumption is that, in our present society, a family's economic circumstances are generally of a higher order when based on earnings than when based on public assistance, since the principal of "less eligibility" underlies the level of benefit payments. The assumption that more income tends to improve the economic circumstances of the family is self-evident; the reason for ranking length of time on welfare may be less obvious. The assumption here is that chronic or long-time dependency contributes to a more deprived level of living than a brief time on assistance. This can be supported by estimating family needs resulting from the inevitable depletion of staples and household stock such as furniture, bedding, and clothing over a period of years on minimum subsistence.

The distribution of the constructed variable appears in Table A.1.

VARIABLE 2: EDUCATION. Many of the households in which the study children lived just prior to placement were atypical of the general population in two important respects: the father or husband was not present in a large number of cases, and several generations were often represented. With varied constellations of persons in the household, and with income in the largest number of cases being public assistance, the designation of one person as "head of the household" was very difficult. In lieu of the educational level of the "head of the household," it was decided to use the highest level of schooling of any adult in the household as the referent for educational attainment characteristic of the households of children. The assumption here is that ex-

TABLE A.1

Variable 1 in Socioeconomic Index:
Main Source of Support

Scale rank	Main source of support	*Percent distribution of households*		
		Child ($N = 329$)	*Mother* ($N = 240$)	*Father* ($N = 129$)
1	Salaries: income $100 per week or more	12	12	21
2	Salaries: income $75 to $99 a week [a]	21	18	39
3	Salaries: income under $75 a week	10	13	18
4	Benefit or alimony payments, help from friends or relatives	12	8	14
5	Public assistance: received for less than 3 years	13	14	2
6	Public assistance: received for 3 to less than 6 years [b]	14	16	4
7	Public assistance: received for 6 years or more	18	19	2
	Total	*100*	*100*	*100*

[a] If source of income was earnings, but amount was not ascertainable, household placed here.
[b] If length of time public assistance received was not ascertainable, household placed here.

posure of the child to a person of higher education is likely to affect his circumstances in a favorable way. For households of the interviewed mothers and the interviewed fathers, however, the actual educational attainment of the mother or father, respectively, was utilized.

The scale on this variable contained five intervals. The highest ranking was allocated to households in which at least one adult had had formal schooling beyond high school. The lowest ranking was given to households in which no adult had gone beyond the sixth grade. The grades included in each rank followed the educational breaks typically found in the American school system. The distribution of the constructed variable is shown in Table A.2.

VARIABLE 3: INCOME RANK OF NEIGHBORHOOD; AND VARIA-BLE 4: JUVENILE DELINQUENCY RANK OF NEIGHBORHOOD. In the study of recreation needs in New York City 74 neighborhoods were ranked according to their median family incomes and juvenile delinquency rates, based on 1960 data.[1] These ranks, from 1 to 74, were utilized to assign scores to the neighborhood of residence. The assumption was that neighborhood conditions were important environmental factors affecting family circumstances. Children, mothers, and fathers were assigned scale scores based on income rank and on juvenile delinquency rank of the neighborhoods in which they lived just prior to placement. A score of "1" on each scale indicated residence in the neighborhood with the most favorable conditions, and a score of "74" indicated residence in the neighborhood with the least favorable conditions. A score of 1 on both scales, therefore, would indicate residence in the neighborhood with the

1. Shirley Jenkins, *Comparative Recreation Needs and Services in New York Neighborhoods* (New York, Community Council of Greater New York, Research Department, 1963), pp. 33–37.

TABLE A.2
Variable 2 in Socioeconomic Index:
Education[a]

		Percent distribution of households		
Scale rank	Education	Child (N = 329)	Mother (N = 240)	Father (N = 129)
1	Formal schooling beyond high school	4	7	7
2	High school graduate	16	21	21
3	Ninth to eleventh grade (some high school)[b]	56	51	43
4	Seventh to eighth grade (some or all junior high school)	8	12	12
5	Sixth grade or less	16	9	17
	Total	100	100	100

[a] Defined as highest grade of schooling of any adult in household.
[b] If educational attainment not ascertainable, household placed here as modal group.

highest median income and the lowest juvenile delinquency rate in New York City. The final distributions of the two constructed variables, with grouped data for ease of presentation, appear in Table A.3.

VARIABLE 5: NUMBER OF NEGATIVE HOUSING CONDITIONS. In consultation with knowledgable persons in the field of housing, a list of 21 items was developed reflecting negative conditions which might exist in dwelling units and buildings in which the study families resided. The list was not intended to be exhaustive, but rather to represent a cross section of conditions commonly found in deteriorated build-

Variables 3 and 4 in Socioeconomic Index:

Income Rank and Juvenile Delinquency Rank of Neighborhood

Scale rank	Neighborhood median income Percent distribution of households			Neighborhood juvenile delinquency rate Percent distribution of households		
	Child (N = 329)	Mother (N = 240)	Father (N = 129)	Child (N = 329)	Mother (N = 240)	Father (N = 129)
1–10	4	3	4	1	1	2
11–20	5	5	5	5	3	4
21–30	3	2	5	6	8	5
31–40	5	3	5	6	5	9
41–50	11	13	11	14	14	9
51–60	22	20	26	15	14	26
61–70	32	35	32	36	37	39
71–74[a]	18	19	12	17	18	6
Total	100	100	100	100	100	100

[a] Note that this grouping includes only four neighborhoods, while all the other groupings include ten. A disproportionately large share of mothers and children resided in these four lowest ranking neighborhoods.

281

ings which could affect the health or safety of occupants. A scale ranging from 0 to 21 was constructed. Those study households rated 0 on the scale had none of the listed negative housing conditions; those households rated 21 on the scale had all of the listed negative conditions. Table A.4 shows a grouped distribution of number of negative conditions existing in the study households.[2]

TABLE A.4

Variable 5 in Socioeconomic Index:
Number of Negative Housing Conditions

Scale rank: number of negative conditions	*Percent distribution of households*		
	Child (N = 329)	*Mother* (N = 240)	*Father* (N = 129)
None	19	13	24
One to five	51	52	52
Six to ten	18	21	14
Eleven to twenty-one	12	14	10
Total	*100*	*100*	*100*

CONSTRUCTING THE FIVE-VARIABLE INDEX. Two problems presented themselves in the combining of the five variables into one socioeconomic index. These were: (1) the ranges of the five variables differed considerably, and (2) the variables were not necessarily of equal importance in reflecting the socioeconomic circumstances of the study households.

With regard to range, the scale on source of support var-

2. In construction of the index the actual number of such conditions reported or observed was utilized.

ied from 1 to 7; the scale on education from 1 to 5; income and juvenile delinquency rank of neighborhood from 1 to 74; and number of negative housing conditions from 0 to 21. In order to derive a single combined score, the first step was to equate the ranges for all five variables by transforming the scores on each variable to standard scores.

The question of values and assumptions, already noted in relation to selection of variables, is also relevant with regard to possible differential weighting of variables in contributing to the index. The decision cannot be avoided whenever more than one component is used. Not to assign different weights to variables is equivalent to assigning equal weights. The five variables, therefore, were considered in terms of relevance and importance to the concept of the index and its hypothetical validity for the study sample —a single score reflecting the socioeconomic circumstances of each family.

Source of support was considered to be the most important indicator of socioeconomic circumstances among the five factors included in the index. Not only was support in itself a critical factor, but the constructed variable incorporated several aspects of support, i.e., source, amount of income, and chronicity of dependency. Consequently, this factor was given a weight of 3 in the index. Education was considered to be the second most important indicator. The educational attainment of the household not only influences the cultural milieu, but also affects and is related to occupation and aspiration level. Education was therefore assigned a weight of 2 in the index. The three remaining variables were all concerned with environmental conditions. Two of them, income rank and juvenile delinquency rank of neighborhood, were highly correlated with each other.

The third, number of negative housing conditions, was considered to be less reliable than the other socioeconomic variables, since it incorporated self-reports of respondents, which may not have been all-inclusive, and interviewers' observations, which were of necessity limited. Since neighborhood factors were external to the immediate family situation and the housing scale reflected "softer" data, each of these received a weight of 1 for the index, or a total of 3 for environmental conditions. The final determination of weights for each variable is as follows:

Variable	Weight
1. Source of support	3
2. Education	2
3. Income rank of neighborhood	1
4. Juvenile delinquency rank of neighborhood	1
5. Number of negative housing conditions	1

The two operations used to produce the final index, standardization of the variables and differential weighting, were accomplished in the formula which follows. This formula was applied to and indexes computed for each of the three sets of households, child, mother, and father.

$$\text{SEC} = 3 \left(\frac{\text{Var}_1}{s_{\text{Var}_1}} \right) + 2 \left(\frac{\text{Var}_2}{s_{\text{Var}_2}} \right) + \left(\frac{\text{Var}_3}{s_{\text{Var}_3}} \right) + \left(\frac{\text{Var}_4}{s_{\text{Var}_4}} \right) + \left(\frac{\text{Var}_5}{s_{\text{Var}_5}} \right)$$

$\text{Var} = $ Variable score
$s = $ Standard deviation
$\text{SEC} = $ Index of socioeconomic circumstances

Examination of the relationships among the variables making up the index was undertaken for the series relating to the sample children's households. This was selected for

TABLE A.5

Intercorrelations of Socioeconomic Index Variables for Children's Households[a]

	Source of support	Education	Neighborhood income rank	Neighborhood juvenile delinquency rank	Number negative housing conditions	Unweighted standardized sum	Weighted standardized sum
Source of support	—	.164	.296	.324	.303	.635	.798
Education		—	.226	.211	.181	.542	.584
Neighborhood income rank			—	.755	.218	.759	.621
Neighborhood juvenile delinquency rank				—	.227	.766	.633
Number negative housing conditions					—	.587	.510
Unweighted standardized sum						—	.957
Weighted standardized sum							—

[a] All correlations are significant at $P \leqslant .01$.

analysis because it was the index representing the largest number of cases (N = 329). Intercorrelations of the five variables relating to the children's households were computed, with results as given in Table A.5.

Although all of the intercorrelations of the constructed variables were significant at the 1 percent level, with one exception they were positive but relatively low. As would be expected, the correlation of neighborhood median income and neighborhood juvenile delinquency rank was high, .755. All the variables were highly correlated with the unweighted, as well as with the weighted, sum of variables. Furthermore, the correlation of the unweighted and the weighted standardized sum of variables was .957, indicating that although the weighting affected the relative contribution of each variable to the sum of variables, the results would not have been very different had the weighting procedure not been used.

There were two main purposes for developing the socioeconomic index: (1) to differentiate within the poverty sample, and (2) to have a quantitative measure which could be related to other study variables. After the index values had been obtained, the numbers in the samples for each of the indexes (child, mother, and father) were divided into three equal parts, and the resulting categories within each were designated as high, middle, or low. The three-category division was convenient for cross-tabulating the socioeconomic scale against other nominal variables in the study, such as ethnic group or reason for placement, as well as against ordinal variables such as attitudinal scores.

Bibliography

Ainsworth, Mary D. *Deprivation of Maternal Care: A Reassessment of Its Effects.* Geneva, World Health Organization, 1962.

Aptekar, Herbert H. *Casework With the Child's Own Family in Child Placing Agencies.* New York, Child Welfare League of America, 1963.

Barnes, Dorothy E., Elaine Bluestein, John J. Cleary, Rosalie R. Garber, Jennifer Marx, Ilene Waxler and Joan Ziegler. *An Exploratory Study into Methods of Evaluating Filial Deprivation.* Unpublished Student Group Master's Project, New York, Columbia University School of Social Work, May 1966.

Bowlby, John. *Maternal Care and Mental Health.* Geneva, World Health Organization, 1952.

Fanshel, David. "Child Welfare," in *Five Fields of Social Service: Reviews of Research,* ed. Henry Maas. New York, National Association of Social Workers, 1966, pp. 85–143.

——. *Foster Parenthood, A Role Analysis.* Minneapolis, University of Minnesota Press, 1966.

——. "The Exit of Children from Foster Care," *Child Welfare* (February 1971), pp. 65–81.

Freud, Clarice. "Meaning of Separation to Parents and Children as Seen in Child Placement," *Public Welfare* XII (January 1955), pp. 13–17, 25.

Gil, David. *Violence Against Children, Physical Child Abuse in the United States.* Cambridge, Mass., Harvard University Press, 1970.

Glickman, Esther. "Treatment of the Child and His Family After Placement," *Social Service Review* XXVIII (September 1954), pp. 279–89.

BIBLIOGRAPHY

Hutchinson, Dorothy. "The Request for Placement Has Meaning," *Social Casework* XXV (June 1944), pp. 128–32.

Jenkins, Shirley. "Duration of Foster Care: Some Relevant Antecedent Variables," *Child Welfare* (October 1967), pp. 450–55.

——. "Filial Deprivation in Parents of Children in Foster Care," *Children* (January–February 1967), pp. 8–12.

——. "Separation Experiences of Parents Whose Children Are in Foster Care," *Child Welfare* (June 1969), pp. 334–40.

——. *Priorities in Social Services: A Guide for Philanthropic Funding, Vol. I, Child Welfare in New York City*. New York, Praeger, 1971.

——, and Elaine Norman. "Families of Children in Foster Care," *Children* (July–August 1969), pp. 155–59.

——, and Mignon Sauber. *Paths to Child Placement, Family Situations Prior to Foster Care*. Community Council of Greater New York. 1966.

Joint Commission on Mental Health of Children. *Crisis in Child Mental Health: Challenge for the 1970's*. New York, Harper and Row, 1969.

Kadushin, Alfred. "Child Welfare," in *Research in the Social Services: A Five Year Review,* ed. Henry S. Maas. New York, National Association of Social Workers, 1971, pp. 13–69.

——. *Child Welfare Services*. New York, Macmillan, 1967.

——, ed. *Child Welfare Services: A Sourcebook*. New York, Macmillan, 1970.

Kohn, Melvin L. *Class and Conformity, A Study of Values*. Homewood, Illinois, The Dorsey Press, 1969.

Loevinger, Jane. "Measuring Personality Patterns in Women," *Genetic Psychology Monograph* LXV (1962), pp. 53–136.

Maas, Henry S., and Richard E. Engler, Jr. *Children in Need of Parents*. New York, Columbia University Press, 1959.

Mandelbaum, Arthur. "Parent-Child Separation: Its Significance to Parents," *Social Work* VII (October 1962), pp. 26–34.

Norris, Miriam, and Barbara Wallace, eds. *The Known and the Unknown in Child Welfare Research*. New York, Child Welfare League of America and National Association of Social Workers, 1965.

Orshansky, Mollie. "The Shape of Poverty in 1966," in *Children's Allowances and the Economic Welfare of Children,* ed. Eveline M. Burns. New York, Citizens' Committee for Children of New York, 1968, pp. 19–57.

Rheingold, Harriet L., ed. *Maternal Behavior in Mammals*. New York, John Wiley, 1963.

Safilios-Rothschild, Constantina. "Family Sociology or Wives' Family Sociology? A Cross-Cultural Examination of Decision Making," *Journal of Marriage and the Family* (May 1969).

BIBLIOGRAPHY

Srole, Leo. "Social Integration and Certain Corollaries, An Exploratory Study," *American Sociological Review* XXI (1956), pp. 706–16.

Struening, Elmer L., and Arthur H. Richardson. "A Factor Analytic Exploration of the Alienation, Anomia and Authoritarian Domain," *American Sociological Review* XXX (1965), pp. 770–76.

Wolins, Martin. *Selecting Foster Parents.* New York, Columbia University Press, 1963.

Young, Leontine R. *Separation: Its Meaning to the Child, the Parents, and the Community.* New York State Conference of Social Work Proceedings 1943–1945, Annual Volume 1945, pp. 52–61.

Index